THREE
NEW
PEOPLE

P9-AFM-238

Praise for
Three New People

"Practical, powerful, and a delight to read. A book like Brian's can change everything for someone who cares."

Seth Godin
Author, *This is Marketing*

"As a magician and entertainer, Brian shares his best tricks of the trade on how to connect. A fun, quick, and worthwhile read."

Shama Hyder
Founder & CEO of Zen Media

"Compelling and practical – *Three New People* offers concrete ideas and examples to help anyone realize the profound potential of everyday interactions."

Ronald Beghetto
Professor and Director of Innovation House
University of Connecticut

"In this highly readable book Brian shares his personal stories and concrete strategies to live a more connected life. As you read, you can quickly see why his TEDx talk has reached over 3 million people and growing."

Conor Neill
President of Vistage, Spain and Professor at IESE
Business School, Barcelona

Miller, Brian.
Three new people : Make
the most of your daily i
2018.
33305240889729
cu   12/23/19

EE
NEW
PEOPLE

Make the Most of Your Daily Interactions
and Stop Missing Amazing Opportunities

BRIAN MILLER

Stay connected!

Visit www.ThreeNewPeople.com for companion resources and videos, and to sign up for Brian's weekly email with tips, techniques, stories, and current research in the field of human connection.

Join the movement on Instagram @threenewpeople

Connect with Brian on Facebook and Instagram: @bmillermagic

Follow Brian's blog at www.brianmillerspeaks.com/blog

———————————————

Copyright © 2018 by Brian Miller

All rights reserved. No part of this publication may be reproduced, distributed, or transmitted in any form or by any means, including photocopying, recording, or other electronic or mechanical methods, without the prior written permission of the author. For permission requests, email the publisher at contact@brianmillerspeaks.com.

All the Things Publishing
www.brianmillerspeaks.com

Ordering Information:

Special discounts are available on quantity purchases by corporations, associations, and others. For details, contact the publisher at the email above.

Illustration and Interior Design: AnnetteWoodGraphics.com

Cover art: Mila Matijašević Babić

Printed in the United States of America

First Printing, 2018

ISBN 978-1-7328447-0-4

For Lindsey, who gave me a reason to listen,
and changed my perspective forever.

Table of Contents

Foreword by Zoe Chance   ix

Introduction   1

I: The Great Big Disconnect

Oh, the People You'll Meet   13

Ed Teaches Me a Lesson   21

The Art of Human Connection   27

How Magic Taught Me the Power of Connection   37

II: A Matter of Perspective

Utilizing Visual Perspective   67

All the Feels   73

Bridging the Gap   83

How to Use Your E.A.R.S.   95

III: New People

The Comfort Zone   125

The Art and Importance of Remembering Names   141

Confidence and Commitment   153

Stop Schmoozing:

A Better Approach to Networking   169

Know Thyself   179

Human Connection is Magic   191

Three New People   203

Foreword

Before Brian Miller was a thought leader, he was a nationally touring magician with a flair for comedy and mind-reading. Do you know the paradox of mind-reading? It's that even though the tricks are the result of clever illusions, in order to persuade an audience you can read minds, you have to be able to read people well enough to actually sort of be a mind reader. That's why magic, and magicians, fascinate me.

The magic doesn't come from the tricks themselves. When you're a nerdy fangirl who's watched hundreds of magic shows, you see many different magicians performing a lot of the same tricks. There are only a finite number of ways to surprise people with limited time and props. Every master will have a unique flair, and occasionally, you see something new and surprising. The first time Brian came to my class at

Yale, he performed a mind-blowing mind-reading stunt that had students forming a chain of psychic links and somehow reading each other's minds. I still have no clue how he did it, but it's not the creativity in the trick that sparked our awe and wonder, it was something else.

What sets a master magician like Brian apart from a good magician is their keen awareness of how to connect through perspective-taking and rapport; planning and conversation. When you master human connection, you earn people's undivided attention, mind and heart, and this is where the real magic lies. Brian's story of perspective-taking to create magic with Ed is one of my favorite stories ever, and the perfect example of what I'm talking about. If you haven't already heard it in his TEDx talk, "How to Magically Connect with Anyone," I won't spoil it; you'll hear about it later in this book.

But you weren't looking for a book on magic, were you? You would have picked up a different book if you were looking for magic tips. You're curious what people like us can learn about psychology and interpersonal influence from a magician. As a muggle who spends my whole life studying, researching, and teaching about interpersonal influence, I can promise you—we can learn a lot from Brian. You'll find tips in this book that sound simple, but they're not easy. Just like when you see Brian toss a mixed-up Rubik's Cube in the air and find it perfectly solved when he catches it, the technique is simple but it's not easy. It takes focus and practice.

Now, you could have bought a book about people-reading from a car or timeshare salesman, but you didn't. My guess is whether you were thinking about this consciously or not, you already realize that what sets magicians apart from compliance professionals and con artists is consent: we *want* to be fooled by magicians so we willingly participate. By allowing magicians to connect with us—to read our minds— we open ourselves to awe. You want to influence people like a magician does. Willingly.

I'm a scientist, and like Brian, I teach interpersonal influence. But here's where a strict focus on science falls short. Even when perfect research studies exist (which is rare in this domain), science can only tell us what's likely to happen on average. However, the people you interact with—your boss, your employees, your customers, your kids, your spouse, your enemies—are all unique human beings. If you learn how to connect with them individually, listening, asking questions, and reflecting on their answers, they will teach you how to influence them. Willingly. And it will *feel like* magic.

Nice to meet you. Now on with the show.

Zoe Chance
Assistant Professor of Marketing
Yale School of Management
October, 2018

Introduction

It's not who you know; it's who you meet.

One day in my early 20s I had to make a 5:00 am flight. Obnoxious, yes, but not out of the ordinary for me. I fly a lot, and I usually fly early. I was at the airport at 3:30 am and, for whatever reason, I was grumpy. My mind was foggy, and my body felt ragged. I hadn't slept much or well in weeks.

Frequent fliers tend to dress the same way for each trip, according to their particular comfort level and needs. My travel clothes were as follows: a pair of slip-on dress shoes (quick to get off and on at security check points), ripped jeans from Express (the ones with the expensive holes), a zip-up hoodie (for varying levels of warmth and quick on/off in tight spots), and my fedora.

Why a fedora?

I was flying to do a magic show, and in those days I always wore a fedora as part of my costume. I used to collect very nice, expensive dress hats, and this fedora was no exception. I couldn't pack it in a suitcase because it would have been crushed, so I had to wear it.

Through the years, as planes got smaller and smaller, I found myself having to take it off just to board the aircraft, and often to keep it off during the flight. So for a period of time I sat with a fedora in my lap on almost every flight.

I got on the plane and checked my boarding pass for the first time, only to discover that I had the very last seat. Have you ever sat in the very last seat of an airplane? I hadn't until that day, and I never have or will again. I got all the way to the back of the plane and realized that the bathroom was *right there*. I could smell it.

Exhausted, sweating, and nauseated, I glanced down at my row to discover that my seatmate was already seated. She looked to be an elegantly-dressed business woman in her mid 30s. She had a black, pixie haircut and a pinstripe pantsuit. She was drinking Starbucks.

And there I stood, a complete and utter mess of a human. Have you ever felt like apologizing to someone as you sit next to them?

I took my seat and almost instantly the pilot's voice pierced through the intercom:

"Uhhhhhhhh folks, here's what's going on."

Frequent fliers recognize red flags quickly, and anytime the pilot wants to chat before the flight is a bad sign. I braced myself as he told us it was going to be a thirty-minute delay because someone forgot to put the wing on (that's all I hear when there's a delay).

I was so miserable I decided to put my headphones on, which is something I almost never do while traveling. As you're going to find out in this book, I love people. I really do. And planes tend to be a perfect place to meet fascinating people from all walks of life. It can be a culturally and intellectually rich experience to chat with strangers on an airplane, and I'm usually all about it.

But that morning I was having none of it.

I started to put my headphones on to drown out the misery when I heard a quiet voice say:

"I like your hat."

I looked up to see the lady next to me making eye contact.

"I'm sorry!" she blurted out. "I noticed earlier when we were in the terminal and thought it would be weird to say that to a stranger, but since we're sitting next to each other I just wanted to let you know that I like your hat. Hi, I'm Zoe."

She extended her hand to shake. What could I do? It was so unexpected that it completely brightened my morning. I shook her hand, introduced myself, and we began chatting.

Inevitably, we ended up having the same conversation you almost always have with a stranger on a plane.

"Where are you headed?" I asked.

"Minneapolis," she said.

"What for?"

"A conference."

"What kind of a conference?"

"Marketing."

"Oh," I said, genuinely interested, "What do you do?"

"I teach influence and persuasion at Yale."

That sounded like the coolest job ever to me! I remember thinking, "There's no way your name is really *Dr. Chance*."

"Where are you going?" she asked.

"Minneapolis," I said.

"What for?"

"A conference."

"What kind of a conference?"

"Entertainment."

"Oh, what do you do?" she asked eagerly.

"I'm a magician."

"Get out!" she exclaimed with Elaine-from-*Seinfeld* like force. "I love magicians!!!"

"No you don't," I said. Nobody loves magicians.

But she insisted, "I teach influence and persuasion! Magicians are kind of my thing."

We chatted about magic, influence, persuasion, and psychology for the entire two-and-a-half-hour flight. As we landed, she asked when I would be doing a public show back in Connecticut. I told her that it was two months away, where it was, and she swore that she would be there.

Sure, I thought. I'm never going to see this lady again.

Two months later, Zoe was right there in the audience. I couldn't believe it. She came up after the show and told me that she *had* to bring me into Yale for a guest presentation.

Yeah right, I thought. I'm never going to see this lady again.

And two months later I was a guest presenter at Yale University, one of the most prestigious institutions in the world.

Zoe and I became friends and colleagues of sorts, and she invited me to do a return engagement at Yale the following term.

A few years later I was invited to speak at a TEDx conference being held in Connecticut. I accepted the invitation and immediately called up my friend Zoe, asking if she would help me write the speech. She had given a TEDx talk before and was familiar with the format.

With her help, I wrote and delivered the talk that went viral, accumulating over 2 million views worldwide in just over a year (now at 3 million in 2018). As of writing this book, it remains in the top 100 TEDx talks of all time.

As my talk spread like wildfire, I began to receive invitations from organizations all over the world to share my magic and sometimes my message. One of those invitations came from Navy Entertainment, one of the few organizations funded by the United States Government to provide, as they called it, "morale, welfare, and recreation" to the American troops and their families stationed on military bases all over the world.

Within a few months I found myself bouncing around Europe, entertaining and speaking with soldiers, sailors, airmen, and marines on naval bases. One of those stops was in Naples, Italy. I had one day off, and my hosts asked if I would like to visit Pompeii.

It's not who you know; it's who you meet.

In case you're as bad at geography and/or world history, as I am, Pompeii is the ancient city that was covered in ash by Mount Vesuvius. Well, I was in Naples; Mount Vesuvius was practically outside my window!

We drove up to Pompeii, paid a few dollars for an all-access pass to wander the city, and after an hour or so we ducked down an alleyway that opened up to a massive outdoor amphitheater.

I looked down and realized I was standing on the same stage in the very spot where, thousands of years ago, my ancestors stood and entertained their audiences.

It was a surreal moment that gave me a sense of my place in the universe. A moment that was emblazoned in my memory. A moment that became a part of me.

It was a moment that only existed because five years earlier, one stranger said to me, "I like your hat."

You have no idea what kind of opportunities await you *just* on the other side of that next connection.

Are you searching for personal happiness or professional success? What about professional happiness or personal success?

You may want to climb the ladder in your current organization or leave that organization completely and take a leap of faith into something new. You may feel lonely and disconnected from those around you, like your friends and family don't really have your back. Maybe you've relocated and find it difficult to make new friends, or you've started a new job and aren't fitting in with your colleagues.

I have been all of those at various points in my life, in one way or another.

Whether your interest in this book is personal, professional, or both, I can assure you of one thing: People who make themselves open to new connections and take the time to nurture meaningful relationships with existing connections will find the world is abundant with opportunities, in and out of the workplace.

If you decided to read this book (and I'm so grateful you did), then you know that something feels off. You can't quite put your finger on it, but society seems more distant and, to be honest, less friendly. What's going on?

Let's figure it out.

You have no idea what kind of opportunities await you.

This book is comprised of three major sections.

Section I, *The Great Big Disconnect,* is exploratory: our terms and goals for connection in an evolving world, how my personal experiences helped me understand the problem, and when I realized that something needed to change.

Section II, *A Matter of Perspective,* is aspirational: how to implement perspective-taking, and a four-step system for mastering the art of active listening. This is the real work on building connections and strengthening relationships.

Section III, *New People,* is practical: a deep dive into concrete strategies and techniques for striking up conversations with new people and reaffirming existing connections.

The Great Big Disconnect

CHAPTER 1

Oh, the People You'll Meet

I read somewhere that we meet and interact with 80,000 people over the course of a lifetime.

Eighty. Thousand. People.

The number stuck with me. There are too many variables between different people's lives to generalize, of course, but let's go with it for a moment.

That means if you are 15, you have already met about 15,000 people. Just turned 30? You've met 30,000.

The question is this:

- How many of their stories do you know?

- How many of their names do you remember?

- With how many of those people did you share a meaningful conversation?

There's a beautiful word you may have never heard before, and that word is 'sonder'. If you've never heard of it, you're not alone. It was invented by *The Dictionary of Obscure Sorrows*, an online project dedicated to creating new words for common experiences we don't already have a word to describe.

What 'sonder' describes is the momentary feeling you get when you see somebody you've never met before—perhaps a stranger walking down the street or standing in line at a coffee shop—and just for a second you realize they have an entire life of their own, completely separate and independent from yours. They have an entire set of experiences, hopes, dreams, worries and concerns that are just as real and vivid as your own, yet you know nothing about them.

You also realize in that moment they are looking at you and thinking the exact same thing. All of those terrific triumphs of yours? All of those awful failures? They mean nothing to that person.

The reason I love that somebody finally invented a word for this experience is that it's so much more common than you would believe. In fact, you meet an average of three new people every single day.

That can't be true, you're thinking.

Well, I have a math degree and finally an excuse to use it. If we accept that you meet 80,000 people in a lifetime and divide it by the average number of years a person lives (78), divided by 365 days a year, that amounts to 3 people per day.

That's three new people, every day of your life, on average. So, I paid attention for a few months to find out if it was accurate (at least anecdotally). To my surprise, three may actually be conservative.

And ever since I realized that, I wake up every single morning asking myself this question:

Will I use those three opportunities today to make my life, and the lives of the people I meet, better?

If you had asked me that question just a few years ago, I would have been forced to say, "No."

The teenage and young adult years of my life were marked by an undeniable self-interest. In high school I obsessed over developing my skill as a magician. My interest in other people existed only insofar as they could function as

You meet an average of three new people every single day.

an audience to test my craft. As I transitioned to college my focus shifted to developing my business as a self-employed magician, and I made sure everyone in my life knew that they came second to my work.

I had many friends and relationships during that time, but none that lasted. Instead I experienced a constantly revolving door of new people who disappeared from my life sometimes as quickly as they came.

Though I was surrounded by people, I was increasingly lonely.

But then I learned a secret, and my life changed forever.

From Loneliness to Personal Success

As a full-time entertainer and speaker, I have been incredibly fortunate to travel the world for over 12 years, sharing my magic and my message with thousands of audiences. I've performed for and spoken with everyone from high school and college students to blue collar workers to corporate executives, soldiers, sailors, airmen and marines, and all those in between.

One of the greatest joys of my job is I am constantly meeting new people. You know that annoying guy on every flight who just wants to talk to everyone? He wants to find out everybody's name, what they do, where they're going, and why?

That's me.

I love people. I never knew I loved people until I started traveling. The long flights, layovers, and table-for-one dining experiences would really wear on me, especially when I first started.

To counter that loneliness, I started talking to people. I would strike up a conversation with passengers waiting for their flight. I would make it a point to find out something about the person behind the desk checking me into the hotel. It became a mission to see how much I could get to know about somebody that I had never met before and would probably never see again.

Can I have a meaningful connection with this person in our 5-minute Lyft ride?

Fractured Perspectives

By the nature of my job, I meet a higher-than-average amount of people. I meet people in airports, coffee shops, restaurants and hotel lobbies, at high schools, college campuses, and corporate offices. These people have different belief systems, backgrounds, cultures, religions, languages, and ideologies.

The more people I communicated with, the more I realized our world is a shared experience. But it's fractured by individual perspectives. You have a perspective, which is different from your neighbor's, which is different from mine.

The fact that the world is made up of so many drastically different perspectives is what makes life such a fascinating and engaging experience. Unfortunately, it can also turn day-to-day living into a frustrating and isolating experience.

Teens: How often do you feel misunderstood by your parents, teachers, and friends?

Adults: How often do you feel misunderstood by your colleagues and bosses?

If you're anything like I used to be, I'm guessing the answer is: "All the freakin' time."

And guess what? Feeling misunderstood leads to loneliness, even when we're surrounded by people.

If that sounds familiar, you're not alone (and that's the definition of irony). A 2018 study of 20,000 Americans ages 18+ conducted by Cigna, a global health service company, found that loneliness has reached "epidemic levels." More than half of the respondents (54%) said that they sometimes or always feel like no one knows them well.

Furthermore, the report states that "Loneliness has the same impact on mortality as smoking 15 cigarettes a day, making it even more dangerous than obesity." That's right: feeling disconnected from the world and those around you isn't just bad for your relationships or career; loneliness is detrimental to your health.

Humans are social creatures by our very nature. It is a universal desire to feel understood. But while so many of us feel misunderstood by our friends and family, very few of us try to make others feel understood.

If you want people to understand you, then you need to learn how to make other people feel understood.

Why shouldn't the "Everyone Feels Understood" movement start with you?

Tuning Out

As if it's not hard enough to connect with people, we now live in an age when technology has overrun our lives. This is an era when we have the ability to instantly interact with people anywhere and everywhere in the world. Yet teens and young adults report feeling lonelier and more disconnected than any generation in human history (Cigna).

I am not anti-technology, and I am not against social media. I quite love my phone. Having immediate access to information and people right at my fingertips is nothing short of amazing. And as someone who travels regularly, being able to stay in touch with friends and family no matter where I am has been a blessing. It

Humans are social creatures by our very nature.

keeps me grounded even when I'm thousands of feet in the air, or thousands of miles away.

The problem isn't that smartphones and social media exist. Even the Cigna study found there is no significant correlation between social media use and feelings of loneliness.

The problem is communication technology has evolved so quickly, and continues to change so rapidly, that many of us haven't learned how to integrate it safely into real human interactions.

In this book I propose a system for making meaningful connections in a world where it can seem like everyone around us is tuning out.

My goal is that you will learn practical and concrete techniques for making better and more meaningful connections with the people in your life. This book is *not* purely theoretical, grandiose, or motivational. These are not just ideas. Yes, I want you to understand why it is so important to connect with others, and how it will enrich your life beyond anything you ever imagined. But I will also teach you exactly how to do it.

As you read this book I ask you to keep one simple thought in mind:

What will you do with your three opportunities today?

CHAPTER 2

Ed Teaches Me a Lesson

When I first started my career in entertainment, I was doing a lot of tableside magic in restaurants. Tricks with cards, coins, rings, strings, dollar bills, salt shakers, napkins —that sort of thing.

I'll never forget this one night that I was on fire.

Have you ever had one of those days when everything just clicks? You wake up and, even though you haven't showered, your hair somehow looks like it was sculpted! Everything you say has your friends or colleagues laughing in hysterics; when the teacher or your boss calls on you, you know the answer right away. You go to the vending machine, put in a dollar, and *two* bags of Skittles come out!

I was having one of those nights as a magician. I was fast and funny; my moves were perfect. I was unstoppable. Teeming with confidence, I swaggered up to a table at which there was an older gentleman and his wife.

"Hey folks, my name's Brian. Would you like to see some magic while you wait for your meals?"

The man looked at me and he said, "Sir, I would love to see some magic, but I can't. Unfortunately, I'm blind."

Several seconds elapsed in silence, which felt like an eternity. I looked at him; I *really* looked at him for the very first time. It was so clear he was blind. His eyes were glazed, and he wasn't really looking at anything in particular. Truthfully, anybody would have known he was blind. But I was so wrapped up in my evening, so lost in my perfect night as a magician, that I wasn't looking at him. I saw just two generic people, and I launched into my show.

I stood there, embarrassed, and that word was ringing in my ears.

Blind... blind... blind...

Have you ever had one of those days when everything just clicks?

22

Eventually I stammered, "I'm sorry, I didn't realize. I don't have anything I can do for you right now."

In an attempt to save the situation, and make myself feel better, I said, "But if you come visit me again sometime, I'll promise I'll have some sort of magic that I can share with you."

"I'll hold you to that!" he announced.

I went on with my night.

A few weeks later they came back in. I recognized them immediately, and I panicked.

I had completely forgotten about them.

I raced by to the room where I kept my props and began pacing frantically. I was wracking my brain thinking of every book I had ever read and every trick I had ever learned. Please, memory, give me something, ANYTHING, that I can do for this man! And then…

I had an idea.

It was an obscure idea. At the time I didn't even know where it came from. But it was all I had, so I composed myself and headed back into the dining room.

I approached the couple and started, "Good evening folks, my name's Brian-"

And he cut me off.

"Alright, we're back!" he exclaimed. "Whaddayagot for me?" he asked with a big ol' smile across his face.

I asked his wife, "May I sit next to you?" She said sure, so I sat down.

"What is your name, sir?" I asked.

"Ed."

"Ed, do you trust your wife?"

"Sometimes."

He had a great sense of humor.

"Will you trust her now?" I asked, chuckling.

"Sure," he said.

I took out a pack of playing cards and handed them to her. I asked her to shuffle the cards and make sure there were no markings or abrasions. She said they were fine.

Then I reached across the table, took Ed's hand, and placed a card in it. I asked,

"Ed, is this a *red* card, or a *black* card?"

He said, "Red."

And he was right. I placed the next card in his hand.

"Red."

Right again. I placed the next card.

"Hmm… black!"

Again, correct.

His wife flashed me a look, confused but intrigued. Her eyes widened as we continued:

Red, red, black, red, black, black, black – faster and faster – *red, black, red, red, black* – he was getting all of them right – *black, black, red, black, red* – straight through the entire deck!

By the end of it Ed was laughing, HOWLING in fact—the entire restaurant was staring at us! I turned and realized that his wife was weeping tears of joy.

It was the most beautiful magic I had ever experienced.

How did he do it?

Simply, I secretly taught Ed a system of communication by which I could let him know the color of the cards, unbeknownst to his wife.

The code, originally created by legendary Los Angeles magician Whit Haydn, is best understood visually. I explained it in my TEDx talk "How to Magically Connect with Anyone," which you are welcome to look up on YouTube if you are curious. Whit published the code in *Stories of a Street Performer: The Memoirs of a Master Magician*.

But the code itself was not the secret. In fact, the code was incidental.

The *real* secret of the trick was communicating the code in such a way that Ed understood how to use it without giving us away.

Connection.

I: The Great Big Disconnect

The *real* secret of the trick was bridging the gap between my perspective and Ed's.

Connection.

The *real* secret of the trick was listening to Ed intently enough to consider his worldview, and his wife's.

Connection.

The *real* secret of the trick was creating a shared experience within which three different people could feel heard, understood, and valued.

Connection.

The *real* secret of the trick,
and of magic, and of life,
is the art of human connection.

CHAPTER 3

The Art of Human Connection

What exactly is a "human connection?"

It wouldn't do very well to write an entire book on the topic of connecting without defining the core term at the outset. After all, feeling misunderstood is precisely what leads to the feeling of isolation and loneliness. Instead of assuming that we are both talking about the same thing, let's agree on what we mean when we talk about human connections.

Words Matter

"It's just semantics!"

Have you ever heard that? It's a phrase typically uttered by someone who is exasperated by an argument.

Semantics is the branch of linguistics that deals with *meaning*. The fundamental question of semantics is: what is the relationship between words/phrases and what they stand for?

In other words, semantics are important. Many everyday arguments between people, particularly between friends and family, are the result of a misunderstanding, and this is precisely because we are *not* clear with our words and what they mean.

Semantics are crucial in building connections because we need to be clear with our words in order to communicate effectively. If you can't communicate with clarity, you will find it very difficult indeed to connect with others.

The real secret of the trick, and of magic, and of life, is the art of human connection.

I witnessed a comedian learn this lesson in the middle of his set. It was my sophomore year of college and as a budding entertainer it was like getting a masterclass in connecting with an audience.

His name was Rob O'Reilly, and at the time he was a New York City based comic who had traveled to upstate New York for a college gig. The show was going great for the first 20 minutes until he launched into a long, story-based joke. All of a sudden, I had no idea what he was talking about. I didn't get the reference point of the joke. I kept laughing because I didn't want to look like an idiot, but as I looked to my left and right I noticed many equally confused students. The laughter slowed to a trickle as the audience collectively agreed that they were confused.

The connection was broken.

Rob carried on for a while, assuming that the joke simply wasn't landing. Eventually, he stopped cold.

"Hey guys, what's going on? What happened?"

Silence in the audience. Nobody, it seemed, could articulate what had happened. Or at least, nobody wanted to. Finally, somebody yelled out,

"What's a 'hipster'?"

"Yeah!" "Yeah—what's a hipster?" The sentiment started to echo around the room.

Rob looked positively confused.

"What do you mean?" he asked. "A hipster. You know, a hipster!"

We just shook our heads. See, it was 2007. While it had existed since the early 1990's in American culture, the term 'hipster,' did not gain cultural significance until the late 2000's. It gained traction initially in cities, like New York City where Rob lived, and which our tiny rural college town definitely wasn't.

A hipster, apparently, is a person who follows the latest fashions and trends outside of the mainstream and the term is often used pejoratively to describe someone who puts more value on the marketing of a product than the product itself. The definition has been widely debated, adding to the confusion.

It's one of those "you know one when you see one" instances. And we had never seen a hipster. Or if we had, we didn't know that's what they were called.

Rob sat down on the edge of the stage and explained this foreign city phenomenon to us upstate college students, which made us feel like we had been let into his world, and thus into the joke.

His clarification let the audience connect with him and made the rest of the show much stronger than it would have been if it had just shrugged off our confusion and barreled forward.

But not all instances of failed semantics have a similarly positive outcome.

Many years ago, before I met my wife Lindsey, I was a lonely self-employed magician going on a lot of blind dates. On one otherwise ordinary evening I sat waiting at a restaurant table for my date to arrive. When she finally did I stood up to shake her hand and introduce myself.

"Hi!" I said.

"Is that how you talk?" she responded.

It completely threw me off.

"Is that how you talk?" she asked again, aggressively.

I had no idea what to say. I started stammering like an idiot.

"I don't understand what you're asking me," I said.

"Like, is that your accent? Is that how you talk?"

I finally answered the only way I knew how.

"This is how sound comes out of my face."

Already exasperated and still standing, she continued, "Where are you from?"

I said, "Buffalo, NY."

She goes, "Well that explains it."

My date meant, "Where are you from" but instead asked, "Is that how you talk?" I was so taken by surprise that I responded defensively as I'm sure you would have. By the time she got to the question she actually meant to ask the first time the possible connection had already broken down.

Needless to say, we never went on a second date.

It worked out for me—I met Lindsey a year or so later. But that's hindsight. Consider how many people we meet and interact with in our personal and professional lives, and how many opportunities are completely missed due to an early failure of clarity.

It's all semantics.

The Meaning of Connection

What do you think of when I say 'connection'?

Some may think of a computer connection, such as a USB cable, which makes for an apt analogy for connections between people. To connect with another person is to establish a link between you and them in such a way that information may be passed back and forth, similar to a cable.

Computers transfer cold data, but human connections go far beyond that. Sure, people can use an interaction to simply exchange necessary information, i.e.

"Hey man, where is the party?"

"It's at 41 West Made Up Drive."

Such interactions are called 'transactional'. You ask for directions, I give you directions. I give you money, you give me a coffee. Purely functional, no relationship necessary. We may as well be computers. (And, yes, jobs based on these kinds of interactions are being replaced by robots, and for exactly that reason).

The majority of our daily interactions are transactional. But human connection is much more than that.

Human connection is the mutually beneficial exchange of emotional data between two people. Both parties are able to give and receive emotional information that serves to build trust and support.

One-sided connections or relationships either fail or lead to emotional abuse. Most of us are only willing to give so much for so long without receiving any emotional support in return. When the emotional information exchange is not mutually beneficial, the connection is broken. It's better for our mental well-being to end relationships that become one-sided.

Digital vs In-Person Connection

Consider our USB analogy again. Computer connections these days may not be physical, but rather wireless, i.e. Bluetooth or Wi-Fi. Similarly, human relationships in the digital age often inhabit a non-physical space. The digital revolution and social media explosion have given us the ability to 'connect' with people all over the world in real time.

How similar are these digital 'connections' to the human connections that we just defined?

In her book *Alone Together: Why We Expect More from Technology and Less From Each Other*, psychologist and

Most of us are only willing to give so much for so long without receiving any emotional support in return.

sociologist Dr. Sherry Turkle argues digital connections provide the illusion of companionship, and that we confuse 'posts' and 'shares' with authentic communication.

I believe it's a difference in degree, rather than in kind. In other words, I don't believe digital communication is a different kind of connection than face-to-face interaction, but it's a much lesser quality. Digital communication is low-res connection, if you will. You can tell it's what you're looking for, but it's not very satisfying.

There is also a generational gap at play. Many older folks, in a criticism of today's youth, are adamant that digital connections do not represent the same quality as connecting with a real person who shares the same physical environment. As you would expect, this kind of accusation tends to prompt a kneejerk reaction from young people that their digital connections are just as valid and, perhaps, even more meaningful than their parents' "old-fashioned" means of connecting.

When it comes to smartphones, the generational gap doesn't just exist between Millennials and their parents: A few years ago, I watched my mother, a fully grown adult woman in her 50s, get chewed out by her mother for "always being on your damn phone."

You can actually trace the argument all the way back to Socrates (yes, the one from that awful Philosophy 101 class), who disagreed with his student Plato about the value of the written word. Plato wanted to write down all of Socrates' teachings, but Socrates railed against the written word, arguing it would eliminate the need to talk to others and degrade the memory.

The debate over the quality of human connection with regard to a new medium of communication is not new. It has existed for thousands of years and will continue to rage on when the next communicative technologies emerge.

In reality it is a semantics debate over the meaning of 'connection'. There are pros and cons to each medium of connection. Those who believe that digital connections are no different than face-to-face connection are having two different conversations, because they have disagreed over the meaning of the word 'connection.'

Any debate based on a fundamental misunderstanding is going nowhere fast.

Still, digital communication is here to stay, and our quest to form meaningful human connections will necessarily take place within such a world. The tips and techniques in this book are optimized for in-person communication but are easily adaptable to the digital world. In fact, the suggestions in my TEDx talk have been shared

There are pros and cons to each medium of connection.

and promoted by social media management companies in blogs about building stronger relationships with customers and clients via social media.

Think about each of your most treasured relationships, personally and/or professionally. Then answer these three questions:

How did you meet, in-person or online?

Do you communicate with this person exclusively in-person, online, or both?

If either of these methods of communication were stripped away, would you maintain the relationship, or would it fade?

Communication will take different forms as the years roll on. If you're reading this book decades from its release, texting and email may already be in the history books. Communicative mediums will continue to evolve, but the tools, techniques, and mindset required to create and maintain meaningful connections will remain.

Why do I care so deeply about this topic?

Let me tell you my story.

CHAPTER 4

How Magic Taught Me the Power of Connection

As a child I was plagued by self-doubt and insecurity. In fact, I had a rather severe speech anxiety. People find that hard to believe now because I make a living on stage, with hundreds of strangers watching and judging me in real time.

My speech anxiety was truly debilitating. I was so terrified to speak in front of people that I found it very difficult to make friends. Class presentations and book reports were the worst of it. Merely the anticipation of delivering the presentation was enough to cause me to feel physically ill. I would end up in the nurse's office, and occasionally be sent home. It was humiliating, and it didn't exactly aid my friendship problems.

Bullies didn't help either. My lack of self-confidence—not to mention my giant glasses, braces, side-part haircut and sweaters—were like a big red bullseye painted on my backside, and the grade school Biff Tannens* of the world would hit the target every time. Like a movie nerd archetype, I was shoved into lockers, beat up, had books knocked out of my hands, and had my backpack stolen routinely throughout elementary and middle school.

And then came high school, and everything changed.

Somewhere around 9th grade I discovered my lifelong magic hobby was a gift, and I began to nurture it. As a result, magic took over my entire life.

Sure enough, after blowing the minds of a few friendly acquaintances, I quickly became known as "the magic kid." It was regularly asked of me, and occasionally demanded of me, to show someone a trick.

"Of course!" I'd say.

Then I would borrow a quarter and bite a piece out of it, only to impossibly restore it moments later. I'd have somebody pick a card and sign it with a Sharpie, only to have it disappear from the pack and reappear inside of a sugar packet! Dollar bills would turn into $10s or $20s at will. Solid objects would be pushed through tables. I even learned how to predict people's decisions before they made them.

---

* That was a Back to the Future reference. If you didn't get it, kindly set this book down and go watch it immediately. Thank me later. Or earlier. Time travel is weird.

Kids would Lose. Their. Minds.

Even teachers were impressed! I would hang after class and during free periods showing my favorite teachers a new trick I had just learned. The principal of the school once invited me to his office and asked to see some magic.

What?!

Each and every jaw-drop reaction fueled my newly developed confidence, which was quickly becoming an ego. I was suddenly popular in the most unlikely way possible. Even the jocks and the "cool kids" wanted to see me do tricks. I started getting invited to parties outside of school, which was uncharted territory on my map of isolation. So long as my pockets were loaded with tricks and I was willing to be a "magic monkey-on-command"—which of course I was—I had friends for a few hours.

I heard the phrase "You're amazing" so many times that it didn't even affect me anymore. People liked me! Or if they didn't like me, they definitely respected me and my gift.

This is actually a pretty common story among magicians. Many kids and even adults get into magic as a sort of "revenge of the nerd," or "revenge of the bullied." Magic can be empowering in an addictive way and even become a coping mechanism that can have some rather unfortunate consequences, as I would eventually discover.

At the time, however, my magical experience was nothing but positive, and I couldn't wait to go away to college to impress people there as well.

That I had invented a new personality for myself became most apparent at the start of my freshman year. I realized nobody at college knew who I used to be. They didn't remember me as the kid who had been bullied, or the nerd, or the teacher's pet. The only person they knew was confident, funny, magic Brian.

I instantly fell into an incredible group of people I believed would be my best friends for life.

Two weeks into my freshman year I suddenly became horrendously sick. I'd never felt so ill in my life. I barely made it to the school's medical center and passed out in the waiting room. I woke up briefly in an ambulance, but then everything went black again. I finally came to in a hospital bed, a nurse standing over me.

"Your friends are here and would like to see you. Should I let them in?"

My friends?

These were practically strangers, none of whom I had even known two weeks earlier. The nurse said they had taken a cab to the hospital and insisted they be allowed to see me. When she told them 'no', they all started writing notes to be delivered to me upon waking up.

I couldn't believe it. I had friends. *Real* friends. I remember thinking my life had changed forever.

My ability to meet and talk to people also turned my academic career into a rousing success. I had always been a good student, but I suddenly found myself pursuing a 4.0 GPA, winning award after award for academic achievement. In retrospect I attribute many of my academic accomplishments to those recently developed people skills: I spent a copious amount of time befriending professors during their office hours, which as an unintended consequence worked in my favor when it came time to file grades. Furthermore, I had lots of friends across many departments who were always willing to help with homework or studying should I need assistance.

Better yet, my romantic adventures took an exciting turn. My new self-confidence made it much easier to chat up girls and subsequently go on dates. Throughout college I was a serial monogamist, jumping from one dedicated relationship to another, usually with no time in between. I was on top of the world: happy, confident, and full of purpose.

But then something happened.

At the end of freshman year, we had to choose our dorm situation for sophomore year: Did I want to stay with my current roommate, choose a new roommate, or ask to be randomly assigned to someone? What a silly question. Of course I wanted to stay with Chris! We had become inseparable over the course of the year. And when I say inseparable, I really mean it.

We watched TV and played video games together almost every night. We played pool and table tennis together at least a couple of times each week. Every weekend we went off campus to do basic shopping, get lunch at the local diner, and occasionally go to a movie. We attended comedy shows on campus and always waited for each other to go to the dining hall.

"Chris! Should I put you down for my roommate next year?" I asked, completely tongue-in-cheek.

"Actually," he replied, "I'm going to room with my buddy next year. Sorry, man."

Even twelve years later I find it gut-wrenching to relive that moment in my memory. I didn't know what to say or how to react. But I didn't want to make it awkward between us, so I think I mustered:

"Oh, okay. Cool."

I stared down at the roommate request form trying to figure out what to do. I had other friends but many of them were girls, and coed rooming wasn't allowed at my school. I had guy friends too, but I figured they would already have their roommate situation figured out. It had never occurred to me to check with Chris because I assumed we were a lock.

So, much to my dismay, I put in for a randomly assigned roommate, and then deliberately buried the awkwardness. I didn't know what it meant and did not yet possess the tools of introspection that I would later develop, which led me to the topic of this book.

Similar strange events (they were always a surprise to me) continued to occur throughout the next three years. As I went back in my memory through four years of college, and sometimes even further back into high school, a pattern emerged, and it was a pattern I wasn't terribly comfortable confronting.

I would befriend someone or get into a relationship. It started off passionate and invigorating but gradually the communication would break down. At some point they would either become increasingly distant or abruptly dismiss me altogether.

And when I graduated college, I was alone.

I'll never forget the realization that after spending four years with what felt like a close community of people, I was beginning my adult life with neither friends nor a relationship. The people who showed up to visit me in the hospital after having only known me for two weeks were no longer a part of my life.

Some of them had unfriended me on Facebook. None of them were talking to me.

It was a huge shock to my system, mentally and physically. I spent many sleepless nights wracking my brain trying to figure out where it all went wrong.

A pattern emerged, and it was a pattern I wasn't terribly comfortable confronting.

The Friendship-Drift Phenomenon

Eternal Sunshine of the Spotless Mind is one of my all-time favorite movies. It is an admittedly quirky but tragic tale of two lovers who, in spite of a deep desire to be together, simply cannot make it work. Frustrated with their relationship and the life they created together, they each undergo a cutting-edge medical procedure to have each other erased from their memories. As the memories fade, each of them looks back on their relationship through the mournful lens of, "Where did something this beautiful go wrong? How did it all come to this?"

Perhaps *Eternal Sunshine* made such a strong impression on me because I watched it at a time in my life when I felt most disconnected from the world: my sophomore year of college.

I had always heard that you meet your best friends for life in college rather than in high school. These are the people that you will share a world and live with for four years, I was told. These are the people with whom you will develop profound and lasting relationships.

When I reached sophomore year and discovered that many of these friendships were drifting, I didn't know how to process the information. I wasn't getting as many invites to the dining hall, or to shoot pool in the rec room. I wasn't met with as much enthusiasm when I showed up to dorm room hangouts.

Sure, people were still friendly with me, but something was different, and at the time I couldn't put my finger on it. It was around this time that I first watched *Eternal Sunshine*.

The main characters in the movie, Joel and Clementine, somehow let their relationship slip through their fingers and dissolve, literally to the point of no return. One scene in particular stuck out. Near the end of their relationship, just before the decision to cut each other out of their memories, Joel and Clementine find themselves lying in bed on a melancholy morning:

Clementine pleads quietly, "I tell you everything. Every damn embarrassing thing. You don't trust me."

Joel replies calmly, "Constantly talking isn't necessarily communicating."

Boy, did that ever resonate with me. Except, it was me who spent all of his time talking, mistaking the constant chatter for communication, and even more so, connection.

At the time I had no idea why my friends were distancing themselves from me. My ego told me it was their fault, not mine. I was great! What was their problem? So instead of spending energy trying to figure out what was wrong and fix it, I simply moved on and found new friends.

Want to take a wild guess at what happened next? You got it.

A year or so later, those new friends drifted as well. So, I found a group of new friends, and pretty much continued on that same cycle through the end of college.

There are only so many times you can watch your relationships crumble before you have to ask yourself, "Am I doing something wrong? Is it me? This can't be a coincidence."

It took a lot of reflection and a long time to admit it, but *it was my fault*.

The people in my life didn't feel like I was invested in them. That wasn't true, but I've since learned that it doesn't matter.

It's not enough to care about somebody. It's not enough to understand them. They have to **feel** understood. They have to **feel** cared about.

I wasn't doing that.

And then, like magic,
I discovered the secret.

The Secret to Meaningful Connections

I recently had the displeasure of watching a magician fumble through his *Ellen* spotlight.

In case you don't know, *Ellen* is the daytime talk show hosted by living legend of comedy Ellen Degeneres. The heart-warming and hilarious show featuring celebrity guests, silly games, and loads of Ellen dancing, boasts 3.9 million viewers per episode—very highly rated in the world of daytime television (Seidman, 2010). To top it off, the show has received 59 Daytime Emmy awards (List of awards and nominations received by Ellen DeGeneres, 2018).

What makes Ellen so special to me is not just that she was a huge inspiration to me when I was a young, aspiring comedy performer. Nor is it that many of my favorite childhood memories with my mother are of watching Ellen's stand-up specials on DVD. Nor even is it that Ellen once uttered the truest thing ever about fear:

"They say the only thing you have to fear is fear itself. Great. Now I'm scared of fear. I wasn't before."

Seriously, how great is she?

No, what makes Ellen so unique isn't any one of those things, wonderful as they are. Rather, it's a quality that distinguishes her among daytime and primetime talk show hosts: her genuine love of magicians.

Talk show hosts seem to be at war with magicians. With the exception of Johnny Carson, hosts generally struggle to maintain their playful, upbeat demeanor when magicians are around. Instead they adopt a more aggressive, antagonistic approach. Go online and search for magicians appearing on David Letterman, on Jay Leno, and even on Jimmy Fallon. With rare exceptions (such as when the guest magician is universally beloved Neil Patrick Harris), the host resorts to heckling the magician in the same way a child yells "It's up your sleeve" even though he's wearing a short sleeve shirt.

Look up "Close-Up Magic Week" on *The Late Show with David Letterman* from 2010 on YouTube. For some reason, David Letterman (or more likely his producers) decided to do an entire week featuring the top close-up magicians in the country. Each night featured a different guest magician, each guest a living legend in their own right. Watch Letterman heckle each and every performer if you want to understand what I'm talking about (and see some absolutely fabulous magic in the process, in spite of Letterman's best efforts to take them down).

But Ellen is wonderful.

She graciously hands over the keys and reacts in a way that suggests she is genuinely delighted and impressed. In short, she's a dream host for magicians.

That is why it is so painful to see someone squander such an awesome career opportunity.

Which brings me back to our Instagram-famous magician and his *Ellen* spotlight. When I say "Instagram-famous," I don't mean a successful magician who later started an Instagram account and developed a large following. Rather, I mean a magician whose entire approach to magic was developed specifically for the medium that is Instagram. In other words, he develops and performs tricks directly to the camera in 60 seconds or less, often set to music and always overlaid with text to catch unsuspecting folks scrolling through their feed.

It's not that magic designed specifically for Instagram and similar mediums is "less than" magic designed for live audiences. Just that it should be performed in the medium it was designed for.

The beginning of our Instagram magician's performance showed promise as he delivered a tight, rehearsed script about who he is (his name), what he does (social media magician), and what we could expect to see (trick with a Rubik's Cube). He was clearly nervous, but perfectly affable.

At 38 seconds into the segment, however, it started to fall apart (at least from my perspective). He asked Ellen to scramble a Rubik's Cube while he mixed his own simultaneously, during which he engaged in this conversation:

"You said you've never done one in your life, ever?"

"Never," Ellen responded.

"We'll try this. Um. Uh. Really, not at all?"

"Never," Ellen answered again, looking slightly agitated that she had just been asked the same question twice within 10 seconds.

"Well, you did a really good job."

Magicians are notorious for saying "good job" or "excellent" after a volunteer completes a trivial task, like signing their name on a card or scrambling a Rubik's Cube. It's our version of "um," but can come off as wildly condescending. I've been as guilty as others.

Our magician then proceeded to show that all of the sides of Ellen's scrambled cube and his were perfectly matched, which is statistically impossible and, truly, a great trick. Unfortunately, he hadn't set up Ellen or the audience to understand the trick, so they had no clue what he had just done or why they should care. The audience eventually started clapping, while Ellen, in an unusual twist, remained relatively stoic. She looked like someone who was on the outside of an inside joke. It was clear to her that the trick was over, but she wasn't quite sure what the trick was.

He went on in a similar manner for over 7 minutes.

What disappointed me about his appearance was not the magic. In and of itself, the magic throughout his performance was quite impressive.

Rather, I was disappointed in his lack of connection with the audience and, more importantly, with Ellen.

Magicians as a community are egregiously bad communicators, and more often than not what separates great magicians from lesser ones is not their tricks, but rather their ability to engage an audience. Magic is a unique performance art in that it requires an audience to exist at all. A dancer can dance for their own enjoyment. A musician can sit in an empty room and lose themselves playing music. But a magician cannot fool themselves, and therefore cannot experience their own magic.

Our magician didn't seem to treat Ellen with humanity. First, he talked *at* her, rattling off a memorized script, without really engaging *with* her. Then he asked her questions whose answers had no impact on the proceedings—it didn't matter what she said, he was going say the next thing he had always planned on saying and do the next thing he had always planned on doing.

Finally, when he did engage her, it was to use her simply as a prop. At one point he asked Ellen to hold a lighter for him. She obliged, of course. A minute later, after stumbling through some more filler words devoid of any content and wrapping the Rubik's Cube in a napkin, he asked for the lighter back.

Why did Ellen need to hold his lighter when he could have simply set it on the table and picked it back up himself?

Surely you've been in a similar situation (minus the magician).

Have you ever been at a party and had someone talk at you for what seemed like hours, while you wracked your brain for either a way into the conversation or a way out of it? They never paused or asked for your opinion, and at some point, you actually started to wonder if they were a new species of human that had replaced breathing with talking.

Now, and be honest: have you ever done that to someone else?

I'm guessing you've both been on the receiving end of this sitcom scenario and been on the delivering end, putting someone else in a conversational death trap with no means of escape.

Why does it happen to us?
And worse, why do we do it to others?

When an Introvert Dates an Entertainer

People are often broken down into two categories: introverts and extroverts.

It's not really that black and white. Most people have introverted and extroverted tendencies, depending on the situation. Still, these labels provide us with a simple way to talk about social interactions.

I had never seriously considered how difficult it is for an introvert to have a conversation in typical social situations until I met Lindsey.

To be honest, I had never considered it at all.

Lindsey is an archetypal introvert. Family, friends, and colleagues would describe her as generally quiet. She frequently finds herself on the receiving end of questions like, "Are you okay?" and "What's wrong?" If you're meeting her for the first time, you probably wouldn't think that she has much to say about anything.

You'd be wrong. Dead wrong.

She, like most introverts, has a lot to say. And it's usually good, *really* good. Lindsey is worth listening to, but extroverts rarely give people like her a chance to be heard.

Hi, I'm a stereotypical extrovert.

I'm the guy who meets everyone on the plane. I'm the guy chatting up strangers in line at the coffee shop. I'm also the guy who talks your ear off at social gatherings without letting you get a word in edgewise. And if you do manage to get a word in while I take a sweet gulp of oxygen (I'm not one of the lucky new species of humans who doesn't require it), there's a good chance I'll cut you off to make a new point of my own.

Or at least, I used to be that guy.

Early in our relationship we had one, big, recurring fight: I had a tendency to interrupt her, and she was sick of it.

In the beginning I had no idea what she was talking about. My family is constantly interrupting and talking over each other like there is going to be a winner at the end of every conversation. That's what I grew up with, so that's how I naturally converse.

I tried to defend myself by citing my family background. I defended my habit of interrupting as excitement and passion. I explained my brain works at a million miles a minute, and I work through my thoughts as I say them out loud.

Eventually I asked in frustration,

"What do you want from me?!"

Lindsey calmly explained she doesn't believe in saying the first thing that comes to her mind. Instead, she needs time to think about what she wants to say and how she wants to say it, so her words are meaningful, considered, and worth putting into the world. Because she doesn't respond instantly, extroverts have a habit of continuing the conversation at such a fast pace that by the time she knows what she wants to say, it's no longer relevant because the topic has changed. To make matters worse, when she *finally* gets a break and starts to share her thoughts, someone usually cuts her off to make a new point.

This is a common pattern of thinking among introverts. Susan Cain has written about it beautifully in her masterpiece *Quiet: The Power of Introverts in a World that Can't Stop Talking*.

So Lindsey, like so many introverts, decided a long time ago that it was easier to stay quiet.

The question remained: What did she want from me?

She wanted me to give her space to think, consider, and respond before I continued the conversation or changed the topic. She wanted me to understand that she wouldn't be so quiet all the time if I would actually give her a chance to engage. Most of all, she wanted me to stop interrupting her when she finally decided that she had something worth sharing.

And there it was.

At long last, we understood each other's point of view, and we agreed to work on it. I focused my energy on getting comfortable with pauses in conversations and slowing down the pace to allow her to consider her responses. I worked very hard to catch myself as I was about to interrupt out of excitement, and instead let her finish a full thought before I added to it.

Introverts make up nearly half of the American population.

Similarly, Lindsey was more forgiving when I didn't quite live up to that ideal, because she understood more fully where it was coming from, and that I was trying.

Introverts make up nearly half of the American population, which means that there are an awful lot of people you talk to on a daily basis that *need* you to work harder at this.

And even if you're speaking to someone who isn't an introvert—wouldn't it be wonderful if we weren't always trying to win a conversation with volume and words–per–minute?

Your challenge for this week is to pay close attention to your conversations. Be aware of how much time you spend talking versus the other person:

> **Are you giving them space to think, consider, and respond?**
>
> **Have you turned the conversation over to them recently to get their opinion or contribution?**
>
> **Do you find yourself interrupting, cutting off, or talking over somebody out of passion or enthusiasm?**

Human connection is a mutually beneficial exchange of emotional data, and it requires a give-and-take.

Being talked at is a complete turn off. You can talk at somebody, but you can't converse at them.

And you certainly can't connect at them.

Connection requires that we create space for each other both emotionally and conversationally.

Magic to the Rescue

What can great magicians teach us about human connections?

There is a classic piece of magic involving three different lengths of rope: a short rope, a medium rope, and a long rope. The magician asks members of the audience to thoroughly examine each piece. The magician then creates the illusion that all three pieces of rope are the same length. Then suddenly, right before your eyes, the three ropes change back into their original lengths: short, medium, and long.

It is a visually stunning illusion that has been around for ages. Most magicians perform some version of it. I've opened my entire stage show with it since I was 17 for everyone from families to high school and college students to corporate audiences and even the American troops stationed overseas on military bases.

> **I have included a performance of this trick in its entirety on www.ThreeNewPeople.com for your viewing pleasure.**

The question is this: what really happens during the rope illusion? It seems like you and I, the magician and the audience, have two very different experiences. But is that the case?

Let's start with me, the magician. What do I see? I see the moves, the juggling, the sleight-of-hand; I see the secret.

But what do you see? You probably see three different ropes changing length impossibly.

That's what we *see* during the rope trick. But what do we *feel*?

As the audience you may feel *amusement*, hopefully *wonder*, and possibly *frustration*. But me? I feel *focus*.

While you witness an impossible moment, I see a simple explanation. While you feel amazement, I exhibit concentration. We don't have two different experiences. Rather, we have two different perspectives of the *same* experience.

A lifetime in magic has convinced me that magicians have a unique dilemma. As the magician, I am the only person who cannot see the magic. Why? Because I know how the trick works, and knowledge of the secret is a limiting perspective. It completely hinders my ability to witness the very magic that I am creating for the audience. So as a magician I must wholly and completely take on the point of view of the audience in order to create wonder.

It seems like an incredible task, and yet we do it on command. Night after night, no matter how many people are in the audience, where they came from, what their jobs are, or what their background is, it always works. To do it, magicians have intuitively mastered a technique called "perspective-taking."

Perspective-taking is the ability to see the world from the point of view of another person.

That's all! It sounds simple in theory, but in practice it can be rather difficult to implement.

Remember our Instagram magician who performed some magic on *Ellen* involving a Rubik's Cube? Well, he's just the latest to pick up on the trend of doing Rubik's Cube magic. While I didn't start the trend, I was one of the early adopters back in the mid 2000s, and I was trained personally by the man who popularized this niche genre of magic, Garrett Thomas.

In every show since my late teens I've taken a Rubik's Cube out of my case and looked into the audience to clearly see that some folks are excited, but most people look angry just because I'm holding one.

I always tell people that there is an easy way to solve it: break the pieces apart and put it back together. You could also take the stickers off, rearrange them, and put them back in the right order. If you really wanted to, you could just smash it with a hammer while cursing loudly. That won't solve the Cube, but you'll feel better afterwards.

Now imagine that I give the Cube a thorough mixing. You can see that it is completely scrambled. Then suddenly, and with no napkins, fire, or other cover, I toss it up into the air and when I catch it, it appears completely solved on all sides.

> **You can also enjoy a performance of this trick at www.ThreeNewPeople.com.**

I've used this trick to secure huge bookings and stun television hosts. The moment the Cube lands in my hand solved, people's jaws hit the floor like a cartoon. It is a reality-breaking moment. People turn to each other in silent disbelief as if to say, "What's real? What's not? We don't know!"

The point is this: Years of performing the Cube illusion have taught me that if I simply take out a Rubik's Cube and, without saying a word, toss it in the air and it comes down solved, the audience is going to think I'm a jerk. Or at the very least, they're going to think I'm a showoff. I don't want them to feel like that! I don't want them to have an antagonistic relationship with me. I want them to *enjoy* the experience of magic.

So, what do I do to avoid that negative feeling and instead create a moment of joyful astonishment? Simple! I make a few jokes. "Take the stickers off, break the pieces apart," etc. When I say that the audience thinks, "Oh, I did that," or "My friends and I did that! We smashed it with a hammer! We threw it at a wall!"

When you, as the audience, have the "I did that too" reaction, you feel like I understand you. And when you feel understood, we make a connection. As a performer, it breaks down the wall between me and the audience. And then I can do the trick, and we can all enjoy the magic in that shared space.

By utilizing the perspective-taking technique through years of performing I was finally able to understand

When you feel understood, we make a connection.

why my audiences were having an *impressed but annoyed* reaction to the Rubik's Cube illusion. Only when I understood where they were coming from was I able to build a performance around the Cube that would delight and produce wonder.

That is also how I realized where my personal relationships had gone so terribly wrong for all those years. On stage I was working very hard to foster a connection with the audience by creating a shared experience where everyone can feel understood, but off stage I was failing to invest the same kind of energy in my relationships.

As I've previously noted, magic cannot exist in isolation. Magic only exists in the mind of each individual person experiencing an impossible moment.

Thus, one of the keys to the success of any magician is listening to the audience. Whether they cheer, scream, weep, or remain silent: what are they 'saying' with their response? How do they feel about the experience that I'm sharing with them? Are they reacting in the way that I expected and desired? Have I created for each person the moment of astonishment that I set out to achieve? If not, what can I do to change that? What can I do to make my relationship with the audience better and more meaningful so that they can experience a moment of beauty, wonder, or joy?

Great magicians leave audiences feeling better about themselves and with a renewed sense of wonder in the world. The finest magicians are able to create meaningful connections because they love their audience truly and sincerely. And when you love somebody, you put their needs ahead of yours. How do you find out what they need? By listening.

That's how it dawned upon me: In my personal relationships, I wasn't listening.

And so, I arrived at the conclusion that my friends and family didn't feel like I cared about them, because I wasn't making them *feel cared about*. I wasn't making them *feel understood*.

"But I do!" I remember trying to convince myself. "I care about my friends! I care about my family!"

After some much-needed soul searching I had a light bulb moment. I realized I could take a technique I had honed on stage and apply it to my life off stage and outside of magic. When I did, I started making better and more meaningful connections with the people in my life. I've made lasting friendships and have shared experiences that will be forever embedded in my memory and deep within my soul. I met a beautiful, fiercely intelligent woman, the love of my life, and I've held on to that relationship. We were married in 2016.

None of that would have ever been possible before.

It turns out that moms everywhere are right: actions really do speak louder than words. You can't just tell somebody that you care about them. You have to show it. You can't just tell them that you understand what they're going through. You have to prove it.

Luckily for me, the key to "showing it" was right in front of me all along, tied to a skill I had already mastered as a magician. Perspective-taking was the key.

The question becomes: How do you implement it?

If you're anything like me (and I suspect that you are), then right now you are thinking back to all the people who have come and gone in your life.

Does it sometimes keep you up at night? Do you mourn the loss or destruction of relationships with a best friend, a significant other, a mentor, or even family? It plagued me for years.

This isn't a book about rekindling relationships that have gone astray. That is not my area of expertise. I too wish I could have a second chance at certain relationships that I once believed would stand the test of time, only to watch them fade away, sometimes as quickly as they came.

You can't just tell somebody that you care about them. You have to show it.

What I **can** share with you is how to prevent it from happening again, how to implement develop profound, meaningful, and lasting relationships with the people in your life, personally and professionally.

The second major section of this book is about how to see the world from another person's point of view, and what to do with that information in order to build connections.

Let's get to it.

A Matter of Perspective

CHAPTER 5

Utilizing Visual Perspective

Perspective-taking is the ability to see the world from the point of view of another person.

But what do we mean by 'see the world'?

To 'see' something is to have a perspective. For our purposes, we will discuss only two types of perspectives: visual and emotional. It's important to understand what each one is, and the difference between the two.

Magicians primarily deal with visual perspective, and it's just what it sounds like.

Visual perspective is how something physically looks to you or another person.

Are you sitting in the living room right now? Your visual perspective is how the living room looks from the position you are currently sitting in. Now imagine that someone walks into the room from the other side, toward you. That person's visual perspective is what the living room looks like to them, walking towards you.

Magicians constantly engage in visual thought experiments. As a magician I must always understand what my trick looks like from the physical point of view of the audience, watching me on stage. Earlier we discussed a classic rope trick, in which three different lengths of rope magically become the same length. In order to convincingly create that illusion, I must be able to differentiate between what I can clearly see—three different lengths of rope—and what the audience "sees"—three identical lengths of rope.

How magicians create the rope illusion is not important; anybody can learn it, and the secret is disappointingly simple. What matters is the dedication that it takes for magicians to constantly and consistently navigate back and forth between their own visual perspective and the audience's.

One of the ways we learn to visualize our tricks from the audience's perspective is by practicing in front of a mirror. It has long been said that a mirror is the magician's best friend. Mirrors allow us to simultaneously rehearse a trick and see it from the point of view of an imagined spectator.

Consider picking an outfit for the day. When you're trying to decide on what to wear, do you ever hold it up to your body? It gives you an idea of how the colors and styles will look against each other, and on you. But just holding it up doesn't always cut it. We often go through the extra effort of trying it on to see what it would look like to an imagined friend, colleague, boss, or date. Have you ever tried on an outfit that you thought was perfect only to discover that the mirror image staring back at you wasn't nearly as great as you believed it would be?

That's the power of the mirror. It reflects back to you a pretty good idea of what someone else would see when they look at you.

But mirrors can deceive you.

Magicians tend to develop a habit of blinking while rehearsing. I mean that literally. While practicing in front of a mirror, during the split second that we execute a secret move (also known as a 'sleight'), our body unconsciously signals us to blink our eyes. When this happens we physically don't see the move, and therefore believe we've executed it flawlessly and invisibly. In essence, it's an exercise in self-deception, and a rather fascinating phenomenon at that.

For this reason, serious magicians began using video recording in order to rehearse. I started recording my practice sessions and all of my live stage shows in 2008. It dramatically improved my work: I discovered that I was terrible. Like, truly awful. I honestly couldn't believe how bad my show was.

You see, video doesn't lie. The camera might add a few pounds, but a camera lens doesn't blink or get distracted.

It isn't influenced by pre-existing beliefs and is not subject to influence or persuasion. The camera captures things as they are, and no amount of denial on your part can alter what it sees.

It's kind of like the first time hearing your voice on a recording when you're a kid.

"That's not me. Oh my God. Is that what I sound like?? I'm a monster!!!"

You're not a monster. Your perspective is just limited by the fact that, well, you're you and not somebody else.

The Star of Your Own Show

Okay, that's great, but what do I do with this information?

I'm so glad you asked. Next time you're in a social situation, whether it's one-on-one or in a group, I want you to imagine that you're the star of a movie or TV show. You've done this before. Don't lie to me.

I want you to 'watch' your conversation from the perspective of a camera filming the scene, capturing you, the star, center screen.

> **Use your imagination to observe the way that you move your hands.** Are they at your side? Are your arms crossed? How does it affect the way that you look to others?

What about your face while somebody else is talking. Where are your eyes? Are they focused on the speaker? Are they darting around the room? If they are, does it make you look disinterested, anxious, or something else?

Take a look at your body posture. How are you standing? Are you slouching or standing up straight? Perhaps you're leaning against something. Is it on purpose? If so, why, and what vibe are you giving off?

Talking is easy. Connecting is hard.

If you're a socially anxious person, this exercise may be off-putting at first. Give it a chance. The goal is to start training your brain to be able to see yourself from a more objective viewpoint; to change that negative anxiety into positive self-awareness.

It is often said that if you want to change your personality (or parts of it), start by changing your clothes. The way you look can drastically influence how you feel, and therefore the way that you act and make decisions.

Learning to create more meaningful connections with people will be difficult, and there's no point in sugar coating it. Talking is easy. Connecting is hard. In order to create better connections, you will need to learn, practice, and hone many skills.

Starting with the simplest of those skills—understanding how to see yourself from your audience's perspective—will get you on the right track. Practice this exercise in your daily conversations for a week or two before moving on to the next chapter, which is decidedly more complicated.

CHAPTER 6

All the Feels

The term "Theory of Mind" refers to a person's ability to recognize that other people have minds that are different from their own. The ability to 'see' the world from the point of view of another person is an exercise in imagination, but it is also rigorously studied and researched by psychologists and neuroscientists. I am neither of those. Therefore, my knowledge of the psychology and science of perspectives is second-hand. Magicians master these skills in an intuitive and practical manner.

Still, I'm a big believer in understanding why something works and not just how it works, to deepen your knowledge of said thing and therefore implement it to the fullest potential.

Other People's Minds

Let's begin with a famous experiment known as the "Sally-Ann test". This is an exercise given to young children in order to determine their ability to see the world from perspectives other than their own. Here is the test as described by neuroscientists Stephen L. Maknik and Susana Martinez-Conde in their wonderful book *Sleights of Mind*:

> "A child is introduced to two dolls, Sally and Ann, and is shown that each doll has her own box, with a candy or toy hidden inside. Then the child is told that Sally is going out for a minute. The experimenter removes the Sally doll from the scene, leaving her box behind.
>
> Next, the child is told that Ann is going to play a trick on Sally. Ann opens Sally's box, removes the candy, and hides it in her own box. Sally returns, unaware of what has happened. The child is asked where Sally will look for her candy." (p. 156)

As you might expect, very young children tend to guess that Sally will look for the candy in Ann's box. This indicates that the child has not yet developed an ability to consider another person's perspective, because the child is looking at the situation from their own point of view, rather than from Sally's. The child knows that the candy is in Ann's box, but does not understand that Sally's perspective is different from their own.

Most older children and adults guess correctly: Sally will look for the candy in her own box, because from her perspective, that is where she left it and would have no reason to believe it is anywhere else.

The "Sally-Ann test" reveals a truth about people that is paramount to the success of magicians and will be crucial to your success in connecting with others.

When Theory of Mind Goes Wrong

Have you ever been talking to someone when suddenly you get the feeling, "This person thinks I'm boring"? What is it that leads you to believe something like that? It could be that the person's eyes are darting around the room, so it feels like they aren't giving you their full attention, and therefore aren't interested in what you have to say. They might be slumped down with their head on their hand, just like a 16-year-old listening to a motivational speaker. They might yawn, which never feels good on the receiving end. They might be giving nothing but one-word, monotone responses, i.e. "Okay," "Hm," or "Interesting."

The fact that you have a theory of mind is what gives you the ability to tune into what another person is thinking, and more importantly, acknowledge the fact that their thoughts might be, and often are, different than yours—even in the same situation.

But your innate ability to recognize that another person's mind is different from your own can also steer you wrong as you start to guess what they are thinking. These guesses, of which we are often rather sure, are informed and shaped by our own pre-existing beliefs and stereotypes that we have developed based on our unique set of life experiences. You typically assume that your intuition is correct and that you have accurately identified another person's state of mind, but you are often wrong. This banter from popular 2000s TV dramedy *House, M.D.* perfectly represents the issue.

> **Cuddy:** "How is it that you always assume you're right?"

> **Dr. House:** "I don't. I just find it hard to operate under the opposite assumption."

We assume our intuitions are correct because to assume the opposite would be exhausting. To make matters worse, we then act upon those guesses as if they were true, which leads to all kinds of complications and misunderstandings.

We often assume we 'know' the minds of people very close to us: spouses, significant others, best friends, siblings, or parents. We spend so much time with these people that we like to think we "know them better than they know themselves." That's why your best friend comes to you for advice! She can't be objective about her problem because, of course, it's her problem. So, she seeks out your wisdom because she trusts that you understand her beliefs and how she generally reacts, thinks, and feels. You can guide her better than she can guide herself. You can be objective.

But in many situations, we're not as good as we think. Nicholas Epley calls it the "illusion of insight" in his magnificent book *Mindwise:* the confidence you have in knowing the minds of close friends and loved ones "far outstrips your actual accuracy." Sometimes we're right, but not as often as we think.

And there's the rub. The false assumption that we truly know the minds of others can get us into all kinds of trouble.

Consider the classic sitcom situation, in which a husband buys his wife a vacuum for her birthday, or as an anniversary gift. The wife is outraged, upset, and offended. The husband can't understand. He knows his wife so well —she's *always* saying that she wants a newer, better vacuum cleaner. She's pointed it out a hundred times!

"I'm such a good husband," he thinks. "I paid attention! Why doesn't she like it? What's wrong with her? What kind of game is she playing at?"

Similarly, the wife is upset because, as far as she's concerned, her husband thinks she doesn't clean enough or keep a tidy enough house.

In sitcom universes, these kinds of misunderstandings result in hilarity. In our real lives, however, seemingly small misunderstandings tend to morph into larger and more complicated problems within a relationship.

A single misunderstanding like this isn't likely to bring down a great marriage,

The false assumption that we truly know the minds of others can get us into all kinds of trouble.

or a close friendship. But many small misunderstandings over time will chip away at even the closest of relationships.

Recognizing that other people have other minds is incredibly important, but it comes with a caveat: the fact that somebody else has a mind completely unique to them, and distinct from yours, means that you will never be able to truly understand their thoughts, feelings, or beliefs.

So, what's the point, then? Is it all for naught? How could we ever hope to make a meaningful connection with another person if so many of our guesses about what's going on in their mind are wrong?

Emotional Perspective

Magicians hijack your natural tendency to guess at what others are thinking, and deliberately lead you down a carefully orchestrated rabbit hole of false information. The fact that I know you are going to try to work out what I'm thinking during a trick means that I can deliberately plan ways to influence your guesses and intuitions about my state of mind.

But while magicians take advantage of your theory of mind in order to fool you (with the larger, more benevolent goal of creating wonder), you can learn to use a similar process to improve your personal and professional interactions.

"Emotional perspective" is one of the most fundamental aspects of interpersonal relationships. As per our agreement, let's be clear about what it means before we dive in.

Emotional perspective is how a person feels about a situation or interaction, typically, but not necessarily, involving other people.

My wife, Lindsey, is a therapist. Therapists are taught the fundamental truth that you can never fully understand someone else's perspective, because you haven't lived through the same experiences as they have. As we've discussed, you can get yourself into all kinds of trouble believing that your interpretation of someone else's perspective is even close to accurate. Of course, it isn't. Our perspectives are shaped by our unique set of experiences, and you *never* share a precisely similar background with another person. There are simply too many variables in life for that to ever be true.

Remember Ed, the blind gentleman I met in the restaurant back in Chapter 2? Let's get back to Ed and his wife. If you recall, Ed and I engaged in an experiment by which he was miraculously able to tell me the color of every single card in the deck, one at a time, even though he was unable to see them. His wife was so thoroughly astonished by Ed's feat that it reduced her to tears. Sincerely, it is a moment that I will never forget.

Before I could create that special moment for Ed I had to ask myself this question: What would magic *feel* like to someone who is blind?

If you accept the premise that we can never fully understand the perspective of someone else, which I do, then this seems like an impossible question to answer.

Here's what was going through my mind: I didn't want Ed to feel tricked. That was very important to me. I don't know, because I'm not blind, but I have to imagine that if I were blind, I might worry that I could be tricked by anybody, at any time. Where a sighted person might delight in the visual splendor of being fooled by a clever magician, a blind person might associate that same feeling with helplessness. At least, that was my thought process. That was my earnest attempt to get into Ed's emotional perspective and make a meaningful connection.

So, I didn't want Ed to feel tricked. Rather, I wanted Ed to feel magic. Even more than that, I wanted his wife—this woman who spends her entire life looking out for him—to see him in that light, and for them to share in that experience together. It was clear from their interaction that she was a crucial part of his world. In some ways, she was his eyes, guiding him through the world and sharing her experiences with him in a way that he could understand.

In that way, it was paramount that she be fooled by my performance. If I did a piece of magic that fooled Ed but not her, she might feel like I had played a trick on her husband. There was something dirty about that idea, and I wanted nothing to do with it.

Those were my intentions. But if I can never fully understand the thoughts and feelings of another person, how do I find a way to connect with someone with such a vastly different perspective? Is all hope lost?

It turns out that there are a number of techniques that you can utilize to bridge the gap between your perspective and theirs.

Be advised: these techniques are not shortcuts. They require practice and dedication into order to use them properly and reap the rewards. *Learning* a technique and actually *implementing* it are two different things, and it is in the implementation that we see results.

Are you ready to implement?

The real work starts now.

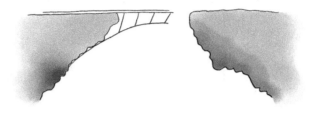

CHAPTER 7

Bridging the Gap

In this chapter I will outline a specific approach to put perspective-taking into practice. These techniques, with practice and repetition, will allow you to better understand the
emotional perspective of other people in any situation. Getting into someone else's emotional perspective sounds sus-
piciously like mind-reading, but it's not. In fact, it couldn't
be further from it.

Ask Questions

The very idea of figuring out how somebody else feels about
our interaction is daunting to many. Sure, we all look for

visual cues to let us know how a person feels—rolling their eyes, sighing, etc. Certain visual cues we take as dead giveaways (even though they're not always), but what's really going on behind those eyes?

Does this person like me?

Should I have said that?

Do they think I'm stupid?

Am I super lame?

We are all plagued by these kinds of questions, some of us more than others. You have undoubtedly experienced insecurity during a social interaction at one point or another. If nothing else, you have certainly laid in bed awake recalling a conversation you had earlier that day, last week, or even years ago, trying to decipher the other person's reaction to it.

Basically, we assume that we are different from the average person—better.

Given everything we've learned so far, how can we even begin to know what's going on inside the mind of another person?

The answer is simple. It's so simple. Are you ready for it?

Ask.

Just ask! Too often we are afraid to ask people questions because we think it will be rude, or that they won't want to answer. But we underestimate people's willingness to answer our questions.

Consider how you feel when somebody asks for your opinion. While some people would rather not volunteer any information, many of us are overjoyed when asked about ourselves.

My opinion on *Batman v. Superman*? I'd be glad to spend three hours giving you my brilliant, detailed analysis!

When someone asks me for my opinion it makes me feel interesting. It makes me feel cared about. It makes me feel like my thoughts, feelings, and beliefs matter to someone else and have relevance outside of my own head.

There's an interesting phenomenon by which we tend to overestimate our own abilities. It's known as the "superiority bias" and "above-average effect" among other names. Basically, we assume we are different, better even, from the average person. When participants in studies are asked to rate their own traits—such as intelligence, driving ability, or trustworthiness—against the average person, most people rate themselves higher than average. And yet, we know intellectually that this cannot be true. Most people cannot be higher than the average. But an individual will rationalize, "Most people are not higher than average, but some are. And I am one of them."

Given that fact, it makes perfect sense to me that we would also see ourselves as different from the average on other topics, such as whether or not somebody would be receptive to answering a question about themselves.

"Well, I love it when people ask me about myself because I'm so confident, but I think most other people wouldn't like it."

Asking questions is the single most direct and effective way to understand the perspectives, thoughts, feelings, and beliefs of another person.

Of course, there are potential pitfalls.

For one thing, you don't know for sure how truthful the person is being in their answers. Suppose your significant other seems angry, and you're pretty sure it's something that you did. Does this conversation sound familiar?

"How are you?"

"I'm fine."

"You seem angry. Is it something I did?"

"I told you I'm fine."

If you've ever been in a relationship, you'll recognize this all-too-common scenario. You will also know just how damaging lying about your feelings can be in the long term.

Another potential problem with asking questions is that people are generally less open and forthcoming with a stranger or somebody they don't know very well than they are with their immediate friends and family, or even close colleagues. You tend to build trust with the people you spend the most of your time with, and because these people have heard more of your stories and been involved in so much more of your personal history, you are more likely to share the answers to questions with them.

So, asking questions isn't perfect by any stretch, but it can still be a very good start, and certainly much more effective than merely guessing based on your own intuitions.

Let's get back to Ed again. I was attempting to create magic for a blind person, something I had never done before. I needed to know more about him before shaping the experience, and so I asked him this question:

"Ed, have you always been blind?"

On its face that might seem like a rude question; Ed and I hardly knew each other! But remember, this was actually our second encounter. The first time we met I fumbled completely, unaware even that he was blind when I introduced myself. Interesting, awkward, or unusual situations can actually fast-track an initial sense of trust due to the shared experience. The second time I interacted with Ed and his wife, it was like we shared an inside joke.

Furthermore, we were in a context that creates a feeling of intimacy: a performance of close-up magic.

Ed's answer was, "Yes, I've always been blind." That was crucial, relevant information to me. I have never been blind, so I don't *know* Ed's situation, but I have to imagine that the perspective of someone who has never been able to see will be drastically different from someone who had their sight, and then lost it to accident or illness. With Ed I couldn't even use the language of sight. He had never been able to see, so he might not have known what I was talking about.

By daring to ask him a personal, meaningful, and relevant question, I was able to adjust my tone, demeanor, and even my language in order to help him feel understood and build that connection.

Don't Be Phony

Please don't read this book and take away the superficial idea that simply asking people questions, any questions, will help you make better connections. Do not Google "conversation starters" and memorize them, to be pulled out whenever you think you need to connect with someone.

People have a built-in "phony detector," and unless you are a professional comedian, actor, or politician, you are probably not capable of delivering rehearsed lines in such a way that they sound spontaneous. Even if you are capable of doing so, the goal here is to make real connections.

You have probably made small talk on occasion with a stranger in line at the coffee shop, on an airplane, in a taxi cab (or a Lyft, if I am to make this book super up-to-date). Those conversations typically go like this:

"Hello."

"Hi."

"So… nice weather we're having."

"Yes, it's lovely."

"…"

"…"

The reason these conversations tend to stall out and die so quickly is that both of the participants recognize a complete lack of genuine interest in each other. The standard "small talk" tropes are so tired that we hardly even hear them anymore. I've been a fly on the wall of many restaurants over the years while working as a magician. Here's a give-and-take I used to hear regularly:

Hostess: "Welcome to The Iron Frog!"

Customer: "Table for two."

These kinds of conversations are the ire of many servers and hostesses. It is disrespectful and shows a complete lack of recognition that the person you are speaking to is a human being.

As an entertainer I give a lot of interviews for local newspapers, podcasts, webcasts, and radio shows. One of my least favorite experiences is an interviewer who runs down a list of pre-planned questions, simply letting you fill in the answers as if it were an online survey.

One of the most common questions I get asked in interviews is, "How did you get started in magic?" Even though

I have answered that exact question hundreds of times, I really try to give a thorough and engaging answer, telling the story as if it was my first time, so as not to make the interviewer feel bad, lazy, or unoriginal for asking a routine question.

Often I will tell the story about how my father and I used to travel from Buffalo, NY to Long Island to visit my grandparents for Thanksgiving each year. My grandfather, affectionately known in our family as Pa, and I would sit in front of the TV and watch the World's Greatest Magic special, marveling together at the tricks, following along at home when they did an interactive piece ("Put your finger on the screen…"), and learning card tricks together out of a magic book. It is one of my most cherished memories.

Upon finishing that story, the interviewer will often nod at me, then looked back down at his list and continue, "So who is your favorite magician?"

What?!

There were so many potential follow-up questions! I pour my heart and soul into trusting this stranger with one of my most personal stories, and all I get back is a check on his list? It is so disheartening, and it completely breaks the spell. Any chance at a meaningful interview, which would result in a much more interesting article, thus benefiting us both, is lost at that point.

Use Relevant Questions to Build Connection

If scripted or pre-arranged questions are unlikely to inspire connection, what will? The key to the "ask questions" technique is to ask meaningful and relevant questions.

Consider Your Shared Environment

Stay present during conversations, whether it is with a stranger you're just meeting for the first time or a family member you have known your entire life. By that, I mean ask questions that are applicable to the current topic of conversation or your shared environment.

If you are trying to start a conversation with a stranger, it is inevitable that you will need to begin with something abstract or general, i.e. "What do you do for a living?" The key is to ask a direct follow-up question related to their answer. Let's imagine a first date:

The Typical Way:

> You: "What do you do for a living?"
>
> Her: "I'm a teacher."
>
> You: "Do you have any siblings?"
>
> Her: "Yes, a younger brother and an older sister."
>
> You: "Where are you from?"
>
> Her: "Florida."

A Better Way:

> You: "What do you do for a living?"
>
> Her: "I'm a teacher."
>
> You: "Oh, what subject do you teach?"
>
> Her: "I teach German."
>
> You: "Wow! Have you ever lived in Germany?"
>
> Her: "Yes! I spent two years there while I was…"

Hopefully you can clearly see how much better the second version is, even though it started out exactly the same way. It doesn't take much to transform something routine like the awkward, initial conversation on a first date, and turn it into something engaging and potentially meaningful. All it takes is staying present, focused, and open to new conversational avenues.

With Ed, the most relevant topic of conversation was his blindness. I know that might sound crude, but it is all to do with context. The context of our conversation was that he and his wife had come back to visit me after I had promised to come up with some sort of magic to share with Ed, in spite of the fact that he was blind. His blindness was the most immediately relevant topic for me to ask questions about because it was the crux of our entire relationship at that point. If we had met at a concert, it would have never occurred to me to ask him about his blindness, because it wouldn't have been relevant, and therefore may have been perceived as rude.

Thus "meaningfulness" is an ever-moving target, and we must remain focused in order to hit it and make the desired connection.

Making People Feel Heard

Asking questions will only get you so far. Even more important is listening to the answers. And even more important than that? Listening to *understand*, not just listening to respond or reply.

You have probably heard this before. It is an old idea that has been passed around in many different formats, perhaps most famously in Dale Carnegie's enduring book *How to Win Friends and Influence People*.

However you may have discovered this idea in the first place is unimportant. What matters is how you reacted to it. If you're anything like me, you probably thought, "That's a good point," nodded to yourself in approval, and then went on with your life, forgetting all about it. So here it is again:

Listen to understand,
not just to respond or reply.

This is the key to making people feel heard, and also where I went wrong most in my life, and I wish I had learned this lesson at a much younger age. It would have saved me a tremendous amount of pain as I lost friend after friend, and ruined relationship after relationship.

Too often when somebody is talking to us, we're only listening so that we can come up with something clever to say, so that the second their lips stop moving we can jump in and say our thing. I'm sure you catch yourself doing that, and if you've never noticed it before, you certainly will now.

Have you ever asked for somebody's name, and instantly forgotten what it was? It's the worst! Do you know why we forget people's names? Because while they're telling us their name, we're thinking about how we're going to say ours! "First name? Last name? Mr. Miller? Put out my hand?" And then you realize that the person just told you their name and you already have no idea what it is. We're not listening! We're on our end of the conversation too often, and we need to get on to their end of the conversation.

When I discovered how badly this was affecting my personal relationships I knew I needed to make a change. But change is hard, especially when it is something that has been ingrained for so many years.

As a result, I created a system to remember to be a good, active listener. I've used it for years, and it runs through the back of my mind in every single conversation, with every person I come into contact with. I'd like to share it with you.

CHAPTER 8

How to Use Your E.A.R.S.

In an effort to be a better active listener I invented, employed, and honed a system to run through during conversations. This system, an acronym that spells out E.A.R.S., at first seemed forced when I tried to put it into practice. But it ended up being a paradigm shift for me.

You may feel taken out of your comfort zone when you first start applying the E.A.R.S. technique, but I promise that with practice and repetition it will become routine. Eventually it will simply become a part of who you are, and you will run through the steps as effortlessly as you breathe and walk.

But first you have to learn what each letter stands for, and how to use them in conversation.

Eye Contact

I'll never forget the first magic trick I ever performed. I was only 4 years old and holding hands with my grandmother as she led me into a public restroom. I grew up before gender neutral restrooms, and mostly before family restrooms! So, naturally, she led me into the ladies' room because the men's room that I was used to was out of the question.

Surrounded by women in a foreign place, and feeling embarrassed about what I had to do, I covered my eyes with both hands and the most amazing thing happened.

I made myself disappear.

Ha! If only, right?

We discover the power of eye contact at an incredibly young age. Babies are more likely to respond positively to someone making eye contact than someone who isn't. By the age of 3 or 4, almost every kid learns to cover their eyes with their hands if they are feeling afraid or embarrassed (The Psychology of Eye Contact, Digested, 2016). Why?

Because if you aren't looking at me, I may as well be invisible.

While engaged in a conversation, the passive participant (the listener) should maintain eye contact with the speaker. (Note: Customs regarding eye contact vary from culture to culture. My remarks should be understood within the context of Western culture. Many Eastern cultures will have these customs reversed, so please be aware of that.)

Imagine you're at a dinner party or a social gathering.

You've made the acquaintance of someone new, and the conversation naturally sparks a story that you think they would enjoy. Let's employ the visual perspective technique from Chapter 5. What do you look like as you tell the story? You, the speaker, are definitely not making eye contact. Your eyes dart around the room as you recall the details of the story you want to relay: What was that person's name? Where did that thing take place? What was the punchline of that joke? Our eyes typically wander as we mentally gather and prepare our thoughts while talking during our half of a conversation.

Every so often, however, our eyes drift back to the listener for a brief moment in order to "check in." If in that moment the person you are speaking to is not making eye contact, how do you feel?

They might be looking down at their phone, or gazing across the room, or staring intently at the menu in a restaurant. I don't know about you, but if I've been telling somebody a story and I notice that they are looking anywhere but at me, it instantly makes me feel like I'm being ignored. I may as well be talking to a wall or yelling into a void.

That feeling of being ignored takes but a second to settle and immediately stacks the odds against making a connection with that person, if not completely destroying it. And here's the kicker: you don't know if they are listening or not, but it doesn't matter. It is possible, after all, that they are staring at the ground in an effort to clear their mind and intently focus on what you are saying, using their sense of hearing alone. You know rationally that they could be doing that.

But emotional perspectives are not rational. The *feeling* of not being heard or understood is supremely powerful.

It matters not what your intentions are. It is your listener's perspective that matters, and that alone. If the person you are listening to feels like you aren't paying attention, whether you are or not is no longer relevant; the bond is shattered.

Imagine instead that in the middle of telling your story, you "check in" with them and find that their eyes are locked on you.

Doesn't that feel better? It looks and feels respectful and attentive, which fosters the feeling of connection.

I am often reminded of a quote typically attributed to Voltaire: "I see you see me."

Of course, there should be moderation in all things. It's quite possible to go overboard. We've all been on the receiving end of way too much eye contact. Use your judgment in the situation. Don't be creepy.

Most of the time the person speaking only occasionally glances at you, so they won't notice how much eye contact you're making; only that you are when they check.

And that's worth everything.

Avoid Distraction

We are too distracted, and it's destroying our relationships.

When I first started doing magic in restaurants at the age of 16, families were simply overjoyed to hear the words, "I'm the magician here this evening." I could see relief in parent's eyes that they were getting a break from constantly entertaining their kids. And I would see the look of excitement in the children's eyes, that they had something to do other than color another placemat masterpiece with the one blue, broken crayon that the restaurant had provided.

Although I no longer perform in restaurants, I have seen the change in attention spans for live entertainment and the disintegration of what passes as socially acceptable behavior. It is largely, if not entirely, the result of smartphones and tablets, which comes as no surprise to anyone. While there is an abundance of anecdotal evidence that smartphones can ruin our in-person social experience, there is finally scientific evidence to support that observation.

In November of 2017, researchers Elizabeth Dunn and Ryan Dwyer from the University of British Columbia in

The *feeling* of not being heard or understood is supremely powerful.

Canada published the results of a study about the effects of smartphone use on the dining experience. They concluded that phones led to a modest but measurable decrease in diners' enjoyment. In short, participants in the study reported feeling more distracted and less socially engaged (Ducharme, 2018).

In the age of instant and personally curated information and entertainment, what once felt like an ordinary conversation can now feel like an extraordinary aberration.

What was once pure joy and anticipation on a child's face at the prospect of watching a magician has now become a pained, "Do I have to? I'm right in the middle of this game," as the parent forces the child to put away their tablet to watch magic. Worse, the parent often resumes playing with their own phone, ignoring their child's first experience with magic completely.

Technology is not going to stop evolving. Social media is not going away. And I don't believe it should. However, like anything in life, there is a time and place for it. We need to make a concerted effort to avoid distractions during conversations with other people.

Part of the problem is that we tend to believe we are good multitaskers. It's a problem because we aren't. Nobody is. Read that again. *Nobody is.*

And I know, I know. You're thinking, "Well, maybe most people aren't good at multitasking, but I am."

Remember that superiority bias we discussed in Chapter 7? That's what is going on here. We all believe that we are better than average. But interestingly, nobody is "better than average" when it comes to multitasking, because almost everybody is equally bad at it.

Studies show only 2.5% of people are even capable of multitasking effectively (performing each task with significantly less accuracy than completing one task at a time), while the rest of us are incapable of doing it at all. And even those lucky few who are able to do it aren't really doing two tasks simultaneously, but rather switching back and forth between two tasks in rapid succession (Kubo & Machado, 2017).

Our inability to multitask is why magicians regularly preach, "Don't talk while you move, and don't move while you talk." The audience can either listen to what you're saying or look at what you're doing, but they can't do both at the same time. From a theatrical perspective this is an important lesson because it means that if you want the audience to listen to your instructions or understand the premise of the routine, you have to stop shuffling cards or "fidgeting," as magicians are prone to doing. But magicians can also take advantage of this fact by deliberately talking at the moment they execute a secret move: it splits your attention. You'll commonly (but not exclusively) see this implemented by comedy magicians. It turns out laughter is a truly magnificent tool for misdirection, as it tends to completely overwhelm the senses. A well-timed joke can literally hide an elephant.

On a more somber note, consider that we've known for years distracted driving, i.e. texting while driving, is qualitatively no different than driving drunk. The studies are clear, and the results are unambiguous (Traffic Safety Facts, 2016).

And yet, we continue to do it.

Multitasking while driving represents a physical threat to ourselves and others. Magicians can convince you that something impossible has happened, simply because you can be so easily distracted.

Why not think of multitasking with regard to relationships in the same way?

We have fooled ourselves into believing we can maintain a meaningful conversation while also watching TV, checking our phone, looking at a restaurant menu, etc. We cannot.

If you want to foster stronger connections with people, whether they are a stranger in a coffee shop or your significant other of 30 years, you need to make a conscious effort to avoid distractions. Give your conversational partner your complete and undivided attention.

When you first make an earnest effort to employ this philosophy in your daily conversations, you will find it is incredibly difficult. We have become so comfortable with multitasking as a way of life that it can feel strained to limit our attention to one thing at a time.

I implore you: try it.

Next time you're ordering coffee, stop checking social media just for 2 minutes while the barista asks for your order. Next time your friend or significant other sits down to tell you about their day, turn the TV off and put your phone in your pocket. Put down the book or magazine. Stop shuffling your damn cards! (Lindsey wrote that last bit).

Be present and attentive.
It goes a long way.

Reflection

There are two distinct definitions of 'reflection' that are relevant to our purpose. Let's start with the more obvious of the two.

The word 'reflection' implies that we should be thinking about, considering, or weighing what a person has just said. And of course, that is always a good idea. However, it's not enough to simply reflect on what they've said. It is all too easy to find ourselves "listening to reply" rather than "listening to understand."

We tend to drift back over to our end of the conversation and start thinking about how we feel about what they've said. I'm not suggesting that we should never consider our own feelings about what someone else has said. Rather, I'm saying that our turn will come, but that time is not the same moment that someone is talking to you.

When you reflect on what somebody has just said to you, be sure to reflect on *what it means to them*.

Why have they just said that thing?

Why was it important for them to share that sentiment?

What kinds of experiences have they had that might shape the meaning of that statement?

Internally asking yourself these questions will help you consider their perspective rather than getting stuck in your own.

That reminds me of the story of the cursed booth.

Restaurant magicians are particularly prone to unusual experiences. Walking up to a table of strangers and asking them if they'd like to see magic is, in and of itself, an odd thing to do. Most people coming into the restaurant are not even aware that there is a magician. It's not hard to put yourself in that perspective. About the last thing you'd expect to hear from someone that you thought was your server is, "I'm the magician." Here's how it plays out:

"Hey folks!"

"We're ready to order."

"Pick a card."

"Rats."

Talk about dashed expectations!

At this one particular restaurant was a single booth, near the bar, that to this day I swear was cursed by the Sanderson Sisters. The fact that it was near the bar is only relevant because I had two regulars who would sit in the same seats at the bar every single Thursday night.

Bob and Sue, best friends, were my biggest fans. Though they were middle-age and I was in my mid 20s, over the years we became close friends as we learned more about each other's personal lives outside of the restaurant. In fact, one of the only downsides to "moving up" in my career was leaving behind my weekly conversations with them, which had become increasingly meaningful to all of us over time.

They sat at the bar with their backs to the cursed booth, but within earshot, and bore witness to what became an impossibly frequent nightmare experience. It became a running, inside joke between the three of us: no matter how many times I tried to engage with people sitting at that booth, no matter who they were, I always failed spectacularly. At best I would be turned away before I began. At worst, well, read on.

Everything was going well that night. People were generally in a good mood. Almost every table was receptive to seeing magic. Most groups were engaged and attentive; there were lots of smiles and plenty of laughter. I've never been a children's magician, but even I have to admit that a child's squeaky, cackling laugh of surprise at a magic trick may be the greatest sound on Earth.

It was a fine night, and I was enjoying myself. And then I saw it: a group of four sat down at the cursed booth. There were two boys who looked about 12 and 19 (but I've never been one to accurately guess ages), and two women who looked about 40 and 70 (and again, who knows).

As I entertained at neighboring tables, I noticed that the boys were craning to watch me work.

"This is it," I thought. "This is the night I break the curse."

I finished with a table and made a beeline for the family. Suddenly, someone grabbed my arm. It startled me as I looked up to see Bob gripping me tightly.

"You're going for it?" he asked, incredulous.

"I'm going for it."

"Good luck!"

To get a better view of my demise, Bob and Sue swiveled in their bar stools ever so slightly towards the booth as I approached.

"Hey folks, how's everybody doing tonight?" I asked enthusiastically, hoping it would catch.

Silence and blank stares from the two women.

"My name's Brian, and I'm the magician here this evening. Would you be interested in seeing a minute or two of magic while you wait for your meals?"

Two enthusiastic nods from the boys. I was in!

"Here I have a clown's nose." I placed the red foam ball on the table, and pushed my finger into it, which emitted a high-pitched squeaking sound.

"It squeaks!" I exclaimed.

The younger boy delighted in trying to squeak the clown's nose as I had, and the older boy delighted equally in the younger boy's failure to do so. I revealed a dog toy hidden in my hand and taught them how to play the same joke on their friends. It was a huge hit.

"Hold onto the clown's nose for me," I instructed the younger boy.

Directing my attention to the older boy, I said, "Now reach into the air and grab an invisible one. Good! Toss it at his hand."

The older boy mimed a throwing action.

"Now, slowly open your hand."

The younger boy opened his hand and as two clown's noses jumped out, an ear-to-ear grin spread across his face. The older boy's jaw dropped. They looked at each other, and then looked instinctively across the table to their guardians, which by now I assumed were their mother and grandmother.

The two women sat stone faced, staring back at the boys' delight with what appeared to be complete disinterest.

Sitting closest to me on the end, the older woman waved her hand like a Disney villain dismissing a peasant, and said,

"I don't believe in magic."

The she took out her phone and started texting. I looked at the mother, who gave me nothing.

I shrugged internally, then shifted my attention back to the boys. Another two moments of magic brought equal enjoyment to them, but I could feel the grandmother actively ignoring us just inches to my right.

"I don't care if she's ignoring me," I thought. "But she should at least be a part of her grandchildren's wonderful experience of magic."

I decided to employ a technique that interactive performers often use to engage a distracted audience member: I directly asked her a question.

"Have you ever seen a magician this close before?"

She didn't look up. I could see now that she was not actually texting. She was furiously typing gibberish into her messaging app. She was button-mashing in an attempt to appear busy.

It kind of blew my mind.

"Excuse me," I tried again. "Have you ever seen a magician before?"

She waved her hand at me without breaking eye contact with her phone.

Wow.

I shifted back to the boys, "Okay, let's do a card trick!"

A woman's voice was heard for the first time.

"Excuse me."

I looked up to see the mother speaking directly at me.

"Yes?" I asked, delicately.

"No one said it was okay for you to start performing."

What?! I asked!

"M'am," my voice quivering, "I asked if it was okay before I started. Both of them said yes."

"He..." pointing at the younger boy, "...is only 12. He is not old enough to make that decision. I don't believe in magic, and I don't wish for my boys to be exposed to it."

Stunned, all I could say was, "I'm very sorry to have bothered you. Have a nice evening."

As I turned to leave I caught the expression on each boy's face. The younger was devastated, clear as day. The older was shaking his head at me, eyes wide open, as if to say, "I'm so sorry. This happens all the time."

I walked back to the bar and rested my elbows against it for a moment to clear my head. Out of nowhere I got that feeling that someone was staring at me. You know how you can just tell? I looked up expecting to see the mother or a manager, but instead was met by Bob's face, grinning like a fool.

"That was awesome!"

That night I found myself asking what had gone wrong. First, and it always seems to come back to this, I wasn't *really* listening to them. I was way too wrapped up in my own perspective; I wasn't trying to connect with them at all. Rather, I was trying to win a game.

Conquer the cursed booth! Break the spell!

This unsuspecting family became an unwitting opponent.

Except, that family wasn't playing a game. As far as the mother and grandmother were concerned, their nice night out was interrupted by a stranger who forced a set of beliefs on their children that ran contrary to their own family values.

It was completely avoidable, if only I had been listening. Upon arriving at the table, I was immediately met with blank stares from the two older women. I did not reflect on why they were being so cold to me, i.e. "Perhaps they are not interested in having me at the table, and I should double check before I start." Rather, I reflected on how I was going to respond to their coldness, "How rude. I will make them enjoy my magic!"

Minutes later when the grandmother waved me off, I couldn't see past how rude she was being *to me*, and so I was unable to recognize how rude I was being *to her*.

In short, my response was selfish rather than selfless. If I had been reflective about how our interaction was being interpreted by them, I could have avoided giving us both an unpleasant experience. I was blinded by my own personal belief that they were robbing their children of the beautiful experience of magic. But that wasn't my decision to make, and that's where it all went wrong.

Paraphrasing is Powerful

I mentioned that there are two distinct definitions of 'reflection.' Here is the second.

'Reflection' also refers to the conversational technique of actively reaffirming whatever someone has just said. After your friend finishes a thought, you can respond with, "So what you're saying is…" and then paraphrase whatever they just said. For example:

> Friend: "*Avengers 2* had too many plot holes."

> You: "So what you're saying is that you wish the movie had paid as much attention to the plot as it did to the action?"

Reflection is an incredibly powerful communicative tool, and it derives its power from its simplicity. The simple act of reflection lets your conversational partner know without a shadow of a doubt that you are fully engaged. Why? Because you cannot do it otherwise. It is impossible to use reflection if you are not really listening, and we all know that. You know what it sounds like when someone isn't properly listening to you. You finish telling a story or making a point, and you're met with a moment of silence while the person you're speaking with recognizes that the noise has stopped. They look up from their phone, the restaurant menu, or the TV, and come out with a dignified:

> "Huh!"

> or

> "Interesting!"

The proclamation is usually met with some intense head nodding, to indicate that they are deeply considering whatever you just said. In truth their memory may be retrieving a few nuggets from their divided attention, just enough to get the gist of what you were talking about. But you know. We all know when we aren't truly being heard or understood.

It's a feeling, and it's powerful.

By occasionally paraphrasing someone's words back to them you indicate that you are present and interested. We all yearn to be validated, and reflection goes a long way.

A fascinating consequence of using reflection is that you discover just how often you have misunderstood what someone is telling you. Sometimes, even though you are actively listening and engaged with whoever is talking to you, you simply fail to understand the point that they are making. Consider our example again:

> Friend: "*Avengers 2* had too many plot holes."
>
> You: "You didn't like the movie?!"
>
> Friend: "What? No, I loved it! I just thought there were a couple of things that didn't make sense."

This is *incredibly* important. In that situation the person you're speaking with realizes that they are not making themselves clear and has a chance to try again, to be confident that everybody is on the same page. Had you not used reflection they would have never known that they weren't making themselves clear.

While practicing reflection, strive to be more like a lake than a mirror. A mirror reflects a perfect image, a copy. If you reflect like a mirror, you'll find yourself being annoying or even confusing people. Like a child who finds joy in repeating exactly what you've just said ("Stop doing that." "Stop doing that." "No, you stop." "No, you stop!" "Mom!" "Mooom!"), it would be rather off-putting if someone was sending your exact words back to you during a conversation.

Rather, try to be like lake. When you catch your reflection in a body of water, you can tell that it's you, but the ripples slightly distort the image. It is reaffirming but by no means perfect.

It's human.

We all know when we aren't truly being heard or understood.

Summarize

The final step of E.A.R.S. is the easiest, and often the most important.

How often do we get to the end of an argument only to discover that we've been *agreeing the entire time?* The trouble is that even after you have intellectually accepted the fact that you agree, the negative feeling of having argued sticks around. We only have a limited amount of emotional currency, and it doesn't replenish nearly as quickly as it drains.

Summarizing is simply using the reflection technique after your conversational partner has finished speaking completely.

After they wrap up their 17-point argument on precisely *why Avengers 2* wasn't as good as *The Avengers*, and before you launch into your counter argument about why sequels always suffer from being compared to the original, and are therefore unfairly judged as being lesser, be sure to summarize their main point.

Ordinary conversations, even idle chitchat, can benefit from summarizing. It's an easy way for both parties to be sure that they are still on the same page. I find that this is especially useful for conversations with friends, family, colleagues, and clients with whom I already have a relationship. The people we continue to converse with on a daily basis (as opposed to strangers we meet once and often never see again) often refer back to conversations from days, weeks, months, or even years ago. Summarizing trains your brain to remember more details.

Imagine that next time your client says, "Remember how I told you about…" and recounts a story she mentioned two years ago at that one dinner event, that you can contribute, "Right! You said you wished that he had…" What a powerful bonding tool!

While I wish all of my conversations with people were agreeable, perhaps the most useful application of summarizing is during an argument.

Tensions flare highest in arguments when one party believes that the other has misunderstood or is misrepresenting their points. That tends to lead to a new argument about the misunderstanding, and the entire conversation spirals from there.

That reminds me of a particularly disheartening conversation at a recent corporate event. I had been hired as a magician to work their cocktail hour, entertaining guests with close up sleight-of-hand magic, followed by a short after-dinner stand-up presentation. The evening was going well until I reached a group with "that guy."

When I say *that guy*, every magician in the world knows who I'm talking about. There is a guy (always a guy) in every single audience, everywhere in the world, who hates magic and can't wait to tell you. I started off strong at that group. People were reacting very well to the magic. We were all laughing and generally having a lovely time. But out of the corner of my eye I kept noticing him. This guy was older, maybe in his 70s, sitting quietly, neither laughing nor participating. I had a feeling he was *that guy* but I hadn't directly engaged with him yet, so I couldn't be sure.

"Sir, may I ask your name?"

"Hmph," he grunted at me.

"… What is your name?" I asked, gingerly.

"No," he replied emphatically.

I looked to the rest of the table, and everyone shrugged their shoulders as if to say, "Yep, he's like that."

"I'm just asking for your name, I'm not asking you to do anything," I offered.

"Magic is stupid. It's not real," he countered.

Oh, I thought. He's the "magic isn't real" version of *that guy*. As a younger performer I would have been completely thrown off by this. Most likely I would have attempted to win him over with magic. But years of experience and many conversations with iterations of *that guy* had led me to a greater understanding of where he was coming from.

You see, people who react negatively to magic are often acting under the pre-existing belief that magicians are trying to make them feel stupid. This is a stereotype of magicians that has been reinforced by thousands of bad magicians, or more to the point, bad performers. And by Jerry Seinfeld:

> "The whole point of magic is to make you feel stupid. Here's a quarter, now it's gone, you're a jerk."

Being aware of the beliefs that led *that guy* to his opinion that magic is stupid allowed me to respond in a meaningful way, with this summary:

"You're quite right, magic isn't real. You know it's not real, because I know how the trick works!"

He looked up, making eye contact for the first time. He clearly had no idea how to respond to someone who was agreeing with him, instead of arguing.

"Magic isn't real, and I'm not trying to convince you that it is," I continued. "But isn't it beautiful that we can make an impossible experience *seem* real, even if we know it isn't. Kind of like a rainbow."

"Hm," he uttered.

I continued on my performance with the rest of the table, and later delivered a fantastic after-dinner show. As I finished packing my things and was preparing to leave for the night, a woman came running up to me.

"Thank you so much; that was terrific. I think Dave would really like to say goodbye to you," she said, gesturing towards the table with *that guy* from earlier.

Oh, I thought. His name is 'Dave.'

Approaching the table, I put a big smile on my face and extended my arm. To my surprise Dave shook my hand heartily.

"It was a real pleasure meeting you, Dave," I said. "Genuinely. I hope that this wasn't too terrible for you."

The woman said, "You know, he watched the entire show. Never looked away."

Dave looked me in the eye and said,

"I just don't understand how magic works. I know it's not real. I know it's a trick. You must have been doing something." He shook his head in disbelief.

Had I misunderstood or misinterpreted Dave's original challenge, that magic is stupid and it's not real, the night could have taken a very different turn. But by recognizing where his beliefs were coming from, even if I disagreed with them, I was able to summarize his main point, letting him know that I did understand what he was trying to express.

It is vitally important to understand the point of view of the person you are disagreeing with. If each side does not understand the point that the other is making they will be forever doomed to shouting past each other. Witness the political discourse on social media over the past couple of years. Regardless of where you land on the political spectrum, the opposite side never seems to remotely understand where you are coming from.

They just don't get it.

You can only have a proper debate, a meaningful conversation about how to overcome an obstacle, if there is some common ground on which you both stand.

Give a quick recap and make sure that they agree with your representation of their point before you respond.

Using Your E.A.R.S. for the First Time

So, there you have it: **E**ye contact, **A**void distraction, **R**eflection, **S**ummarize.

Eye contact makes your conversational partner feel that they are being heard. Avoiding distractions will help *you* stay focused on what is being said. Reflection confirms to them that you are absorbing the details rather than just getting the gist. Summarizing is the final conversational checkpoint to avoid miscommunication and unnecessary arguments.

E.A.R.S. is a practical way to stay engaged in every conversation with absolutely anyone that you meet. You will find that this seemingly simple system not only breeds connections, but it also decreases your self-conscious tendencies in social situations. We tend to lose ourselves in our own self-centered concerns:

We tend to lose ourselves in our own self-centered concerns.

Does she like me?

Should I have said that?

Did they think that was funny or find it stupid?

Did I just mispronounce that word?

Why is he looking at my hair?

The natural consequence of active listening is that it focuses your mind on the perspective of others, rather than on your perception of yourself. When all of your energy is channeled into truly understanding what someone else is saying, there's simply no room left to worry about how you look or sound.

In that way, it benefits all parties.

Still, it needs to be said that E.A.R.S is simple in theory but challenging in application. For many, including myself, it represents a complete shift in how we approach our daily interactions.

But I really encourage you to try it out.

Learning to use my E.A.R.S. has made me a better magician, yes, but more importantly it has made me a better friend, son, and husband. In short, it made me a better person.

But a thought may have occurred to you by now:

"Wait... I can't make a meaningful connection, or any kind of connection for that matter, until I've already started talking to somebody. Forget perspective-taking. Forget asking questions. Forget E.A.R.S!

How do I even *start* a conversation?

New People

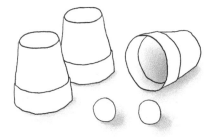

CHAPTER 9

The Comfort Zone

You've made it this far. You're committed to creating a better world in which we can all feel heard, understood, and valued. You want to spread the message that "our world is a shared experience" and live a life according to those principles. You're more eager than ever to meet three new people tomorrow.

But how do you start?

You cannot wait for someone else to help you feel understood. You're going to have to do it for them. And they may not reciprocate right away, or even for a while. We get back what we put out into the world, so let's put it all out there.

Pick a person, one person, any person, today, and strike up a meaningful conversation. The only way to discover the hidden opportunities in your daily interactions is to connect with people beyond a surface level, which requires stepping outside of your comfort zone.

What Exactly is the Comfort Zone?

When we hear about the comfort zone our entire lives, what are we always told to do?

Get out of it!

We are always told to get out of our comfort zones. It makes the Comfort Zone sound like an awful, terrifying place. It must be, otherwise we wouldn't constantly be told to leave. And yet, no one ever tells us what it is. No one ever really defines it.

Your **comfort zone** is a set of routines that keep you at ease.

That's all it is. In fact, studies have shown that staying in your comfort zone decreases stress and promotes well-being.

Wait, what? That sounds like a fantastic place—Netflix and sweatpants for life! Why would you ever leave a place like that?

You already know why. While it does increase stress, getting out of your comfort zone is also what allows you to grow as a person. When we step even a little bit outside of our standard routines we find ourselves in new situations that challenge our system, which leads to the development of new coping skills and resiliency.

If you've never been exposed to a germ your body has no defense mechanism to handle when you inevitably come into contact with it. Similarly, your ability to handle whatever life throws at you is directly related to your wealth of experiences, and we only get new experiences when we step outside of our regular routines.

While it does increase stress, getting out of your comfort zone is also what allows you to grow as a person.

Getting Out of the Comfort Zone

Interestingly, and perhaps somewhat counterintuitively, we need to feel safe in order to be productive outside of our comfort zones.

Psychologists refer to this as "optimal anxiety," which is a heightened but safe state of anxiety brought on by a new or challenging experience. Operating under optimal anxiety increases performance effectiveness and efficiency. In other words, stretching outside of your comfort zone is beneficial. Reach too far, however, and you might crumble under the stress. Too much anxiety can be debilitating.

Leap out of an airplane, but take a safety class first and wear a parachute.

The key to finding a balance is to approach new or uncertain situations under controlled conditions.

That's why it's easier to meet new people if you're out with friends. You get to take a leap of faith by chatting up a stranger, but land safely with your friends if it doesn't work out.

It's for the same reason I work very hard to treat audience volunteers in my magic shows with the utmost respect. It is not within anybody's comfort zone to go on stage and help a magician during a magic show. They must feel completely alone. What's going on in their mind? Let's employ our perspective-taking technique here.

In order to volunteer in a magic show, you have to believe the magician is going to keep you safe. Take my show, in which I invite at least five volunteers on stage over the course of 70 minutes. Being a comedy magician, and a particularly silly one, I have to imagine my audiences trust I'm not going to put them in harm's way. But they don't *know* that for sure. Plenty of magicians have performed dangerous stunts. Heck, magicians have died on stage, and audience members have been hurt in the process.

So, they must first trust that I'm going to keep them safe from harm, physically. More importantly, however, they have to trust that I'm going to keep them safe emotionally.

At a public show, any potential volunteer is probably in attendance with friends, family, or a significant other. These are all people that they will continue to see on a regular basis, which means that anything we do on stage will have a lasting impact for them. As the entertainer I am unlikely to see anybody from the audience again. It's wonderful when I do (shout out to my true fans), but rare. It's easy to forget that if, off-the-cuff, I call somebody a silly name, their friends may continue calling them that name for years, as an inside joke. And it's completely conceivable that, not wanting to seem like an uptight person, they play along with the joke even though they would prefer not to be called that name.

In other words, something that lasts seconds and means nothing to me could have long term repercussions for a volunteer.

Given that I mostly work for private events like company holiday parties and corporate banquets, there is a good chance that every single member of my audience will continue interacting with everyone else in the room in their daily work life.

If I poke fun at Betsy from accounting, she may have to endure similar taunts from everyone else in the office on a daily basis. That could be annoying for her at best and humiliating at worst.

If, instead, I take care of my volunteer, treat them with respect and dignity, and gently guide them one step at a time out of their comfort zone, then by the time they go back to their seats they will have had a completely new and unique experience that can be treasured for a lifetime. Furthermore, the (admittedly silly) experience of successfully helping a magician in front of an audience of strangers teaches you that you're capable of something you might not have even imagined was possible.

That lesson is invaluable. And the more often we learn it, the stronger we become.

In *The Icarus Deception,* Seth Godin writes about the difference between a "comfort zone" and a "safety zone." One place keeps you safe, while the other makes you feel comfortable; they are very different places. The goal is to align your comfort zone with the safety zone.

What happens when the safety zone moves, but we don't realign our comfort zone with it?

Complacency.

The *safest* thing you can do in a world where personal and professional success is increasingly built on connections is to meet new people, gain new experiences, and develop resiliency. But what's *comfortable* is to do none of those things.

We have an obligation to ourselves to stretch, reach, and tip-toe outside of our comfort zones. More than that, I believe we have a moral obligation to encourage others to step into a new safety zone with us, even if it's uncomfortable at first.

When I strike up a conversation with a stranger in a way that makes them feel safe to converse with me, I move outside of my comfort zone and they respond in kind.

Suddenly, our comfort zones both shift. We are now each a little bit more comfortable meeting new people.

The zones realign, and we both win.

Conversational Safety Nets

New experiences are fundamental to learning and growing. But even world class trapeze artists practice new stunts with a safety net until they have developed the confidence and skillset to go it alone.

For us non-circus folk, a safety net often comes in the form a friend or family member engaging in the new experience with us. I recently had the pleasure of helping a man who has climbed five of the seven summits, including Everest, prepare for his TEDx talk. I learned that his safety net came in the form of an (expensive) highly trained and experienced expedition team to guide him up the mountain.

A card trick may not change your life in a meaningful way but getting on stage in front of hundreds of strangers, colleagues, friends, or family will most definitely add to your ever-evolving list of "things I can do and survive."

The longer that list, the more resiliency you develop, and the more likely you are to try more new things in the future. Who knows? Helping a magician may be the push you need to take that advanced class, apply for that promotion, or ask out that special someone.

But what is your safety net when you're alone in public and want to make a meaningful connection with a stranger?

There are so many opportunities on a daily basis to experiment with stepping outside of our comfort zones. Three of those daily opportunities come in the form of new people to connect with.

One of the reasons we tend to shy away from talking to strangers is because we simply don't know what to say. What do we talk about when we finally muster up the courage?

We talk about the weather or the traffic. These are conversational safety nets: topics of conversations that are so standard, so automatic, so boring that absolutely anybody can comment on them regardless of their background.

Many of my colleagues who speak and write about "talking to strangers" argue against these sorts of banal topics. But there is nothing egregiously wrong about bringing up the weather. If you are particularly shy and wary of opening up to strangers, talking about the weather or the traffic is actually a great way to ease into a conversation.

But the odds of sparking a meaningful connection by talking about the weather are slim to none.

Not because of the content, but because of the follow-through: talking about the weather rarely *leads* anywhere.

Why not?

Because we can never think of a really good follow-up question when somebody says,

"Boy, it sure is hot outside."

Instead of responding, "Right?" or "I know!" consider this:

"What kind of weather do you prefer?"

That may lead someone to describe a place they used to live, after which you might learn a little about their past. Or they may describe a place they visited once that they'd like to retire to someday, in which case you will learn a bit about their hopes and aspirations.

Or: "What do you like to do when it's this hot?"

Here we will discover some of their hobbies and preferences, giving us a better picture of who they are outside of the Starbucks line, gas station, classroom, or wherever you're meeting.

Questions like these also tend to prompt reciprocal follow-up questions and give you a chance to either bond over a shared preference or discuss your different preferences. Real conversation!

**Visit www.ThreeNewPeople.com
for an additional resource,
"Meet Your Three:
7 Ways to Open a Conversation with Anyone."**

But what if you are downright afraid of rejection? What if you've tried to open a dialogue with strangers before and been shut down?

What if you're terrified of failure?

Learn by Failing

We tend to avoid situations that have previously gone badly, particularly if those situations evoke a feeling of embarrassment, shame, or rejection.

It's hard to ask somebody out after being rejected, for fear it might happen again. It is with trepidation that we open up to a loved one about a sensitive topic, for fear of being mocked, or worse, dismissed.

Understandably, it can be difficult to strike up a conversation with a stranger, for fear of being brushed off or ignored completely.

When I first made a conscious effort to make meaningful connections with the three new people I interact with on a daily basis, while also deepening my existing connection with friends, family, and clients, I didn't suffer from a "fear of failure" the way that I did before my career in entertainment. Very few people outside of world class athletes and the military are trained to push through failure the way that performing artists are. Young entertainers learn often and early to fail with grace. We succeed not in spite of failure, but because of it. The best way to hone an act is to shine a light on its shortcomings, and the only way to do that is to fail in front of live audiences.

In my pre-entertainment days I was terrible at handling failure. I had an awful speech and social anxiety. By middle school I had stopped trying to make new friends because I had been mocked and bullied so badly for so long that it just didn't seem worth the effort.

I first learned to handle failure and rejection by doing magic tricks that I occasionally goofed up. I was so desperate to be a great magician that I instinctively started using failure as a motivating tool.

Here is the story of my earliest professional public humiliation.

I was 17 years old and performing my first-ever stage magic show. It seemed an impossible feat to be able to entertain and fool over 100 people at the same time. Unlike close-up magic, there was nowhere to hide. When you work an event as a strolling magician, you get to blend in with the crowd, just trying to engage a few guests at once. I felt much more in control of my environment and material in close-up settings, as I could move this way or shift that way and issue instructions to conform the audience to my needs.

On stage, however, you're naked. I mean, you may as well be. Everybody can see everything you're doing at all times, and they sit from an objective vantage point. Backstage before the show I remember thinking, "If I screw up, the entire audience will see it." That was very different from my prior experience in strolling magic, where a mistake would only be witnessed by two or three people, rather than the entire room.

"Please welcome BRIAN MILLER!"

And with that bellowing announcement, there was no time left to worry. I walked on stage with a big smile and started the show. To my surprise, it wasn't that bad! I was nervous but having a great time. The audience was appreciative and receptive. Everything was going as planned.

Famous last words.

The time came to perform a classic of magic, perhaps *the* classic of magic: the cups and balls. The trick is thousands of years old and began as a game in which a ball is placed underneath one of three cups. The cups are mixed around and the participant has to guess which cup contains the ball. The ball impossibly jumps from one cup to the next, appears and disappears at will. But the end of the trick always contains a big surprise: typically, a large object appears unexpectedly under one of the cups. It is quite common to see a piece of fruit, like a lemon or a lime.

I had decided to use a potato. I guess I thought that was funny.

The potato had been sitting in my right jacket pocket since the beginning of the show, unbeknownst to anyone. I arrived at the moment when I needed to sneak the potato underneath the cup. The audience was completely distracted by something else I was doing, but only for a split second. Magicians live in these tiny, pressure-filled windows of opportunity.

Before I finish the story, I have a confession: I had never worn that jacket before. In fact, I'm not sure I had ever worn *a* jacket before!

As I tried to get the potato out of my pocket it got caught on the lining of the jacket. With but a fraction of a second to make a decision my brain rattled around all of the different options, and this was the solution it came up with:

Yank the potato with all of your might.

I did just that.

I YANKED the potato as hard as I possibly could. It cleared the lining and, with tremendous momentum, shot out of my hand. The potato sailed through the air in the shape of a beautiful, majestic rainbow, hit the stage, and rolled all the way across it while I and the entire audience watched it in silence.

Finally, I turned back to the cups and finished the trick, without the potato.

Then something amazing happened: the audience had no idea I had screwed up. Remember your first piano recital when your teacher told you, "If you mess up, don't make a face. The audience doesn't know what the song is supposed to sound like"? Magic relies on the element of surprise! The audience didn't know the potato was supposed to show up underneath the cup. For all they knew I planned that moment of absurd comedy, where in the middle of this elegant, classic of magic, I performed the (now infamous at that particular school) appearing, flying potato trick!

That failure was of tremendous benefit to me because I learned that if I could come out the other side of a monumental public embarrassment and continue performing, then I could survive pretty much anything. Imagine if I had stopped doing magic because of one embarrassing result!

And yet, that is precisely what we do when we fail to connect with someone. "Welp, I tried. Got shut down. That's enough of that." There is something very personal about being rejected or ignored that cuts us deeply. Rather than motivating us, it tends to deflate us and steer us away from future attempts.

Loneliness has reached epidemic levels, and it has the same impact on mortality as smoking 15 cigarettes per day. Loneliness is killing us. We cannot afford to give up trying to connect with others (Cigna).

If you take nothing else away from this book (although I hope that you take plenty), please take this:

Your experiences, not your results, define who you are.

As I built my career I gave a lot of great shows, plenty of mediocre shows, and at least a few train wrecks. The same goes for my relationships, in and out of work.

I wish I had a truly awesome or hilarious story about trying to connect with a stranger and failing, but I don't. Not because I don't fail—of course I do. But when I try to strike up a meaningful conversation and it doesn't work out, nobody really notices

Your experiences, not your results, define who you are.

except me. Nothing really happens. It doesn't make for a memorable story.

Failing to connect with a stranger is like is a flying potato in the middle of a magic show. We go, "What the heck was that?" Then we shrug it off, move on to the next thing, and quietly learn from the experience. It is the experience, not the result, that matters.

Still, you don't need to reinvent the wheel. There are tried and true techniques that can be utilized to safely step out of your comfort zone, limit your failures, and start making connections.

The next chapter contains
one of the best.

CHAPTER 10

The Art and Importance of Remembering Names

Some years ago, my mom drove in from Maryland to see me do an open-to-the-public magic show on Long Island. It had been a few years since she had seen one of my shows, and I felt like it had improved drastically since the last time she saw it, so after the show I asked, "What was your favorite part of the show?"

To my surprise, her answer wasn't a particular trick, joke, or routine.

Instead, she said, "I can't believe you remembered everybody's names, from the beginning of the show to the end."

My mom was referring to the fact that throughout the show I have at least five volunteers helping me out with a variety of tasks. Being an interactive show, and with my entertainment roots in comedy clubs, I will over the course of the night refer to earlier volunteers, referencing things that had happened while they were on stage. In comedy it is known as a "callback." Callbacks are a great way to give the show a sense of immediacy, especially in a show like mine that is meticulously scripted.

Yet, she wasn't impressed with the callbacks themselves, but rather with the mere fact that I remembered each volunteers' names as I called back to them. Even in the final minutes of the show, I made a callback to someone from the very first piece over an hour earlier.

"Brian," my mom said, "I can't remember anybody's names. It's such a gift that you can do that."

It was the first time I had ever given it any thought: I guess I do a pretty good job of remembering people's names. The more I thought about it, however, the more I realized it wasn't a gift. Rather, it was a skill that I had been developing, unconsciously, over many years of giving interactive stage performances.

Upon deeper consideration it became clear why such a skill had developed without my being aware of it: names are eminently personal and convey a sense of familiarity.

There is a traditional saying in the entertainment industry: *if the audience likes you, then they will like anything that you do.*

If there is one thing I try to avoid, it is failing before I've even begun.

Why Names Matter

Earlier, in Chapter 7, I asked if you ever learned somebody's name and immediately forgot what it was. There was more weight to that question than I initially let on.

Names are a funny thing.

Have you ever turned your head at the sound of your name coming from a different conversation, even though you were confident that it wasn't intended for you?

There's a phenomenon by which you can selectively focus in on your name, even in the loudest and noisiest of environments. It's called the "cocktail party effect," a reference to the cacophony of conversation and music that engulfs the average cocktail hour. You may not be consciously aware of it, but if you think on it now, you'll realize how quickly and easily you respond to your name, even in such trying environments, like a sports stadium or at a rock concert.

I'll say it again: names are a funny thing.

On one hand, they are completely arbitrary. Your parents assigned you a random string of letters at birth that, when pronounced aloud, create a sound that amounts to nothing more than a variable in mathematics: it points at something. Your name (probably) isn't even unique. Most of us are given a first name that has already been given to hundreds of thousands if not millions of people.

Take my name, "Brian." A quick Google search reveals that there are 1.2 million people in the United States alone with the first name Brian, and 1.3 million with the last name Miller. Even put together, there are over 5,000 people in the U.S. with the name "Brian Miller"—there were seriously 3 of us in my high school at the same time.

Yet we are very attached to our names. "Brian Miller" is not just my name; *it's who I am*.

You might even associate a particular meaning with your name, especially if you have a religiously or culturally significant name, i.e. 'Matthew' is Hebrew for "gift from God". But it could simply be that our name, particularly our first name, is the one thing that, from birth, always remains constant.

That's why it is so crucially important to remember people's names.

Be it your personal or professional life, people are genuinely impressed when you remember and use their names. It is perceived as a sign of respect and creates an immediate sense of familiarity, which in turn facilitates trust and bonding.

We *really* care when someone forgets our name, and we are pleasantly surprised when someone remembers.

If I've only met you once, briefly, and you remember my name upon our second encounter, I would be genuinely taken aback. It would make me feel special, like I must have at least made a small impact on you. That would give me a very positive feeling about you in return, which would set the tone of the entire conversation to follow.

In that way, the mere act of remembering and using someone's name can be a critical first step in forming meaningful connections.

Techniques for Remembering People's Names

As far as I'm concerned, I am an entertainer first and a magician second. As an entertainer, the first order of business is to get the audience to like me. I need them on my side because the success of the entire show depends on it. I need you rooting for me. I need you to feel like *my* success is *your* success (or more to the point, *our* success).

After my mom inadvertently led me to that lightbulb moment of realization, I began to look for ways to apply the ability to remember people's names that I developed as an entertainer to my life off-stage.

Just like the "perspective-taking" technique we discussed in depth, name memorization is a skill that can be learned, practiced, and honed. There are many books and resources available to you to study memory techniques in depth, but here are a few of my tricks and tips for improving your ability to remember people's names.

Use Your E.A.R.S.

The straightforward, easiest way to remember somebody's name is to actually listen when they tell you what it is. Get out of your own head, stop thinking about how you are going to say your own name, look up from the restaurant menu, put down your phone, etc. Focus solely and completely on them as they give you their name.

Remember that they are *giving* it to you. It is a gift.

We only give out our name in two situations: when we want to form a positive relationship with someone, and when we have to. Sometimes you have to give out your name, such as when the barista asks for it to complete your order, the receptionist at the doctor's office needs it to verify your appointment, or when the police ask for a statement.

Other than that, we are often hesitant to give away our name unless we are emotionally invested in the person, or open to the prospect of connecting with them.

If you treat names like a gift you will be more grateful for receiving them, and you will find yourself taking better care of them.

The Rule of Three

One of the oldest tricks for remembering someone's name is to use it out loud three times in quick succession. In the context of my live stage show, it goes like this:

Me: "What's your name?"

Him: "James."

Me, shaking his hand: "James? It's very nice to meet you James, thanks for helping me out with this. [To audience] James and I are going to..."

It looks excessive when written down, but you would be surprised how naturally it flows. This is a technique you can immediately implement in social and professional settings. If it feels weird to hit their name three times rapid fire, try just twice while you're learning the technique, i.e., "Sue? It's nice to meet you, Sue."

That alone should help lodge their name into your brain, and it's the technique that I use most frequently.

When you get comfortable hitting it twice, try this: "Sue? It's nice to meet you, Sue. Sue, what do you do for a living?"

It looks much worse written down than it actually flows in conversation. But you don't need to take my word—go test it!

Amazingly Awesome Alliteration

Remember these from school?

"Please excuse my dear Aunt Sally."

"Every good boy does fine."

"Thirty days has September, April, June, and November..."

Mnemonic devices are mental shortcuts we use to easily remember large pieces of information.

A phrase like "Please excuse my dear Aunt Sally" is known as an **acrostic**: a phrase where the first letter of each word comes from an acronym.

An **acronym** is a word, real or invented, made up of the first letter of each word from a phrase.

For example, PEMDAS is the *acronym* made from the *acrostic* "Please excuse my dear Aunt Sally" to help you remember the order of operations in math, i.e. **p**arentheses, **e**xponents, **m**ultiplication, **d**ivision, **a**ddition, **s**ubtraction.

Another example is "Every good boy does fine," which you learned as a young music student so that you could remember the order of the notes in the Treble Clef: **e-g-b-d-f.**

You know by now that one of my favorite acronyms is E.A.R.S., which you remember stands for **E**ye contact, **A**void distraction, **R**eflection, **S**ummarize. I particularly love E.A.R.S. because it doesn't just create a random series of letter, but a proper word, 'ears,' that is related to the very thing the acronym is meant to help you remember: active listening.

While acronyms are a terrific memory device, they don't help much when it comes to remembering names.

But alliteration does.

Alliteration is the process of putting multiple words in a row that all start with the same letter. Meet a Susan with a big smile? In your head say, "Smiling Susan!"

When Lindsey I were just dating, years before we were married, I was introduced to her entire group of friends at a dinner party in one shot, rapid fire. I got all of their names in one take and never forgot them. I think it even surprised Lindsey when I remembered all of their names a few days later during the course of conversation.

Ask for Spelling

One of the techniques I use regularly on stage is to ask for somebody's name, then immediately ask them to spell it.

> Me: "Hey, thanks so much for helping out. What is your name?"

> Him: "Brandon."

> Me: "Brandon – can you spell that for me?"

> Him: "B-r-a-n-d-o-n."

> Me: "Ah! Brandon, not *Brendon*. Got it. Brandon, please stand right here for me."

I find that visualizing the letter-for-letter spelling of someone's name in my

The easiest way to remember somebody's name is to actually listen when they tell you what it is.

mind makes it infinitely easier to recall later. Spelling it out in my head makes the name a specific image, rather than just a word.

It also gives me a chance to utilize the aforementioned repetition technique. Pairing up two or more of these techniques will dramatically increase your ability to remember their name.

Write It Down

Lastly, never underestimate the power of writing things down. I am not afforded the opportunity to do this as a performer, but I use it regularly in my personal and professional life off-stage. I have found it is always a good idea to keep a notepad handy.

After you've just met somebody and are now walking away, quickly jot down their name and any other important pieces of information. Examples include: where you met them, where they are from, their job title or role, the company they work for, and any personal information they mentioned, such as spouse name, kids names/ages, hobbies, etc.

I discovered the memory power of writing things back in college. While studying for an exam, I would copy my notes from the entire chapter by hand over and over again. It is well documented in the psychological community that the act of writing something down seems to imprint the information. It takes something that was merely verbal and adds both a kinesthetic and visual element. Your brain now has three associations with the information instead of just one.

I used to keep a small notepad and pen in my back pocket, or inside jacket pocket, at all times. Now I use a smartphone with a built-in stylus for a digital notepad that is always accessible. If you don't want to carry a notepad and your smartphone doesn't have a stylus, you can always use the native note-taking app within your smartphone to type out a quick reminder message.

Of course, the act of remembering someone's name will not guarantee success or seal a business deal. No single technique in this book will do that on its own.

Success itself is far too complicated to be achieved by a single tool or idea, as we are about to discuss.

CHAPTER 11

Confidence and Commitment

The road to success is a labyrinth with many locked doors in its path. But there is always at least one person who holds the key for each door.

It would serve you well to be kind to this person.

Sincerity Can't Be Faked

I'm not suggesting you pretend to like people in order to get something out of it. Like pessimism, it simply doesn't work. Remember, people have a built-in phony detector.

You can't fake sincerity.

Rather, I am suggesting you make an honest and genuine effort to make a connection. Not exclusively with those who hold the specific key you want at this moment, but with everybody you meet, all the time.

Success is never a straight line; it is a maze. It is only looking backwards that we can connect the dots and establish a clear path from where we started to where we are now. What that retroactive path never shows is all of the moments in between the dots. It never shows all of the people you met, and all of the interactions you had, that created the opportunity for you to find your way.

"Treat the janitor the same way you treat the CEO."

This quote has been making the rounds on social media over the past few years, and it has no clear original author. It may be a takeoff on a quote that is often attributed to Albert Einstein:

> *"I speak to everyone in the same way, whether he is the garbage man or the President of the university."*

Or this quote, often attributed to Malcom S. Forbes:

> *"You can easily judge the character of a man by how he treats those who can do nothing for him."*

Regardless of its origins, the idea is simple to understand: Treat everyone with respect, dignity, and kindness, regardless of who they are or may be, or what they can or may be able to do for you.

I told you my story in the Introduction about meeting Zoe on a plane to illustrate the larger point about why it's worth talking to strangers: you never know who it is you're talking to. But that story, told by itself, glosses over an important fact, which is: the hundreds or thousands of conversations I've had with strangers that started and ended with a single meeting, and did not turn into a life-altering series of events.

When you realize you will have to put that level of energy into each and every conversation you have, knowing the vast majority of them will not lead to any reciprocity or 'help' you on your path to success, you start to appreciate that success via connections *is only* achievable if you truly believe in it. You might fool one or two people into believing that you care about them when you don't, but you cannot fake a lifelong commitment to a philosophy of making meaningful connections.

This commitment is what I call *Three New People.*

Treat everyone with respect, dignity, and kindness, regardless of who they are or may be, or what they can or may be able to do for you.

It takes a lot of guts to try to make a meaningful connection with a stranger, let alone three new people every single day. You are bound to be on the receiving end of many eye-rolls and brush-offs. People are not as receptive to the idea of communicating with strangers these days, particularly in America.

How to Develop Confidence

In my experience, the key to overcoming these kinds of interpersonal hurdles is confidence, pure and simple.

I am reminded of a talk I attended when I was 16 years old. My best friend Adam and I convinced our parents to take us to a magic lecture. Neither of us had ever attended such an event before. We had no idea that the lecturer was a living legend of mentalism: Max Maven.

While describing the workings of a trick involving playing cards, there was a moment when Max showed a card and then handed it to a volunteer, face down, having secretly switched it for a different card. From that point forward the success of the piece rested entirely on the volunteer believing, without a shadow of a doubt, that the card they held was still theirs. A magician in the audience of the lecture raised his hand.

"But what if they turn it over and see that it's not their card?" he asked.

"They won't," replied Max, matter-of-factly.

"Why not?"

Max sighed, "I'm now going to give the answer that garners many angry emails the day after my lecture. Do you really want to know why they won't turn over the card?"

"Yes!" shouted a bunch of magicians.

"They won't turn over the card," Max continued slowly, "because I don't want them to."

And there it was. The secret to the trick was not the sleight-of-hand. It wasn't even the misdirection. It was confidence. Max had a commanding control over the room and his audience. He set the rules for the show through his presence, words, and actions. An audience volunteer in a Max Maven show would never even consider turning over the card.

"But I'm not confident," I can hear you saying out loud, to yourself, right now (boy, are my ears good).

Luckily, faking confidence is indistinguishable from actually being confident.

The same cannot be said for sincerity. Perhaps the reason you can fake the former but not the latter is that confidence is an internal state; whereas, sincerity is external. In other words, confidence is something you feel about yourself, while sincerity is something that others feel about you.

How I Developed Confidence out of Necessity

Necessity truly is the mother of invention. This story is going to blow your mind.

Two companies agreed to sponsor me at the age of 22, resulting in a professional wardrobe that cost nearly $3000, at no cost to me, ever.

Let me make this clear: I was not yet a successful magician. In fact, I was barely making ends meet. And yet a men's clothing company gave me nearly $3000 worth of clothes—dress shirts, slacks, suit jacket, and garment bag—plus custom tailoring on two pairs of slacks, in exchange for mentioning their name on some of my promotional materials. Furthermore, anyone who dropped my name was offered a whopping 40% off of anything they purchased!

Similarly, one of the oldest dress hat companies in America gave me two hats free of charge, and a steep discount on future hats I wanted to purchase, also in exchange for plugging their company occasionally in my promotional materials.

Entertainers in my local region came out of the woodwork to ask how I managed such a deal, let alone two. They must have believed I possessed kind of golden business advice, or alternatively, I was supremely lucky.

I didn't know how to tell them neither was true. The real secret? How did I land two big sponsorships at 22 years old?

I asked.

We have already discussed at length the advantage of asking meaningful and relevant questions in order to make connections. Sometimes, however, asking questions is just the straight line between two points: A) What you want, and B) getting it.

What did I want? I wanted some nice dress clothes to wear to events and impress prospective clients, but I couldn't afford anything that wasn't from Walmart (and even that was out of the budget). So, my manager and I hatched a plan: we would pitch the owner of a local men's clothing store a plan to sponsor me and give me free clothes.

Of course, it wasn't quite that simple. We had to give him a reason to give me free clothes. What did I have that he could benefit from? Promotion! That's right, I actually believed that my career at 22, when I was doing at best four low paying, local events per month, could actually benefit the owner of a successful men's clothing retail business.

"I have a website!" I exclaimed. "I can offer them promotion on my website. I'll mention their store as a sponsor."

My website in those days attracted maybe 20 people per month. And 10 of those were probably coming from my own family and friends checking in on me. What I'm trying to say is that our plan was dubious at best, bold at least, and downright stupid at worst.

But sometimes the naivete of youth works in your favor. We worked up all of our courage and waltzed in to his store one day, unannounced. We asked to speak to the owner, who definitely thought he was about to make a sale. Au contraire!

He was about to be sold.

"My name is Brian Miller," I nervously began. Then, pretending I wasn't nervous at all, I continued.

"I am a full time professional magician. I work at events all over the region. I'm looking for a sponsor for my business."

"Sure, man. What were you thinking?" He responded calmly.

"I'm thinking a full wardrobe," I said with pure adrenaline. "Five or six shirts, two pairs of slacks, tailored, a sport coat, and an overcoat for the winter."

He grinned.

I thought, "I'm in!"

In retrospect I realized that grin was one of pure entertainment, the kind a parent has after having just watched a child make a list of ridiculous demands.

"Well," he started. "I do like supporting local businesses. Is there anywhere I can see you perform first? I can't sponsor you if I've never seen you work."

A fair point.

"Yes, there is. I can get you tickets to my show at Foxwoods."

"Oh." His face shifted to genuine interest.

For context, Foxwoods Resort Casino is the largest casino in North America. In Connecticut and throughout New England it is very famous. Working at Foxwoods was about the best currency an entertainer in my region could have hoped for. I was opening on off-nights for a veteran performer.

"You have a show at Foxwoods?" he asked incredulously.

"Yep, at the comedy club. How many tickets do you want for this Sunday's show?"

We reserved four tickets so he could bring up to three guests and figured we had the sponsorship locked down.

That Sunday rolled around, and I nervously scanned the audience before the show.

He never showed up. I searched the crowd during my 30-minute stage act hoping he'd come in late, but no dice. After my show I went backstage, depressed. But my manager cheered me up.

"He just walked in, as you were finishing."

I pulled myself together, put on my best confident-face, and headed out into the room. As we approached his table, he started apologizing.

"I'm so sorry, man! The girls were running late. You know how girls do."

I didn't. I was 22. But I managed something like, "Yeah! Girls, am I right?"

He had three scantily clad women on his arm, and I remember thinking how popular he was. My manager, 10 years my senior and much more versed in the ways of the world, had a laugh explaining the situation to me later.

"Any chance you can show us something when the next act is over?" he asked.

"Of course," I said. "Enjoy yourself tonight!"

Later when the main act ended I made my way over to his group.

"Alright!" he exclaimed. "Show us what you got!"

I took out a single sponge ball (the red squishy foam balls every magician uses) and asked him to hold onto it. Then I plucked an invisible ball from the air and mimed tossing it at his hand. When he opened his hand, two sponge balls popped out.

"Whoa!"

I'll never forget the grin that spread across his face as the women started laughing uncontrollably.

"You got it man," he said as he extended his arm for a handshake. "Come on in Monday and we'll get you all set up."

I shook his hand, thanked him, and walked away. He had no idea I had spent the last two hours crafting a perfect 20-minute demonstration designed to win him over.

Suffice it to say, when Monday rolled around we sealed the deal. Just like magic I had a complete, professional wardrobe and my first ever sponsorship. We brought a friend who owned a local media company to get a quote from the owner of the store and write a press release. That press release made its way into Connecticut's newspaper, which I pushed out across my digital platforms.

A few months later I was agonizing over a new fedora I wanted to buy but was too expensive.

"Why don't we pitch that hat store in New Haven to sponsor you like the clothing place did?"

What a great idea! Our approach to the hat store was similar and even easier. See, having one sponsor already made convincing the owner of this generations old hat store, a fairly simple task.

"They gave you that overcoat?" he asked, wide-eyeing my jacket.

"Yes. And a complete wardrobe."

"That's a nice coat. Okay, you've got a deal. We'll give you two hats under $150 each."

A handshake, a photoshoot, and one press release later sealed the deal.

From then on, I learned to fake confidence in my personal life and professional life. It is a very similar strategy to Harvard professor, researcher, and TED celebrity Amy Cuddy's work on "power posing"—the idea that if you pose like a superhero (chest out, hands on hips, head held high) for two minutes before going on stage, into a presentation, important meeting, or job

Acting confident makes you confident.

interview, your body produces more testosterone and less cortisol (stress level).

Acting confident makes you confident.

How can you practice acting confident?

Imagine you're at a social gathering and a confident person walks into the room. What do they look and act like? They probably have their head up high with a big smile on their face. They move about the room with purpose rather than aimlessly wandering, choosing what to do and who to engage with next. They're walking towards you now, hand outstretched. As they introduce themselves, notice how they speak with power. Not loudly, just clearly and with intention.

Next time you're in public, at a social gathering, or attending a work function, emulate that confident person you just imagined. You'll impress yourself with the results.

We've already discussed eye contact at length, and here it serves us again. We tend to perceive people who make eye contact as attentive and engaged, which makes them appear confident. And when someone seems confident we treat them like they are. So, if you make eye contact with a conversational partner, or even a stranger across the room, you'll be perceived as having confidence and get treated as such, which in turn will actually make you feel more confident. It's a beautiful self-fulfilling prophecy.

You might also consider how you are dressed. Have you ever put on an outfit, looked in the mirror, and instantly thought,

"Yes! Today I'm going to conquer the world." Studies have repeatedly shown that the clothes we wear can make us feel more powerful (Slepian, Ferber, & Gold, 2015) and even increase attention and intelligence (Adam & Galinsky, 2012). Imagine yourself in an interview wearing pajamas. Feeling confident? Of course not. Now imagine that same interview wearing a custom fitted suit from your dream clothier. Huge difference, right?

Humans Love to Help

Beyond learning that confidence is key, my experience landing sponsorships and other major career accomplishments brought about another lesson I have taken to heart and embedded in my life's philosophy: you have no idea what people may be willing to do for you unless you ask.

Humans have a deeply ingrained instinct to help each other. We are, after all, a social species. At a biological and sociological level, the survival of the human race depends on our ability to socialize and work together. That fact has been studied in great depth and written about extensively. I highly recommend *Social: Why Our Brains Are Wired to Connect* by Matthew D. Lieberman.

Think about how hard it is to say 'no' to your friend when they ask for a ride to the airport, or to help them move. Furthermore, have you ever agreed to do a favor, even though you really didn't feel like it? Now think back: after you helped somebody out, didn't you feel good that you did it? I'm sure the owner of that men's clothing store did after helping out a young, aspiring magician. Why else would he do it?

We get an immense satisfaction in having helped out a fellow human being, even in a small way.

I'm not suggesting you take advantage of people's difficulty saying 'no' to requests and favors. Rather, I'm saying you should go out of your way to say 'yes' to favors asked of you, and in turn you should feel comfortable asking others for things you want. If we all help each other out, we all benefit.

My friend Alok, a beautiful and giving human who is also my web designer, recently mentioned on his blog that he is more willing to give time to someone who wants to "pick his brain" when they offer something in return, such as an introduction to a new potential client. Some readers interpreted his position as, "Never help someone who cannot offer something of value to you." I read his post with a much more optimistic interpretation:

We all have something of value to offer, regardless of our socio-economic situation. Let's trade so that everybody wins.

If you do ask for help from someone, it's a good idea to offer something in return, whether it's a service you provide or mentioning their business as I did with the clothier and the hat store.

What we often don't realize is that while somebody else may hold the key that unlocks the door in front of us, we hold the key that unlocks the door in front of them.

Oh, by the way, let me answer the question you've been wondering ever since I mentioned Foxwoods: How did a punk 22-year-old, inexperienced, starving artist magician ever manage to land a gig at the largest casino in North America?

I asked.

CHAPTER 12

Stop Schmoozing: A Better Approach to Networking

When I first met Lindsey she said, "I could never do what you do." She didn't mean magic.

She meant networking.

Like many people Lindsey has a visceral aversion to what she calls 'schmoozing.' It's the kind of ego-stroking, phony, out-for-yourself approach to meeting new people that you typically see at networking events.

In case you're not familiar with the term, a **networking event** is an organized social gathering folks attend with the intention of adding people to their network of contacts.

Undergrads, grad students, and business professionals are frequently encouraged or required to attend networking events on a somewhat regular basis in order to build up their list of people they know. The basic idea is the more people you have in your network, the more doors are potentially open to you as you build your career.

Theoretically it's a great idea. In practice it's a mess.

Most networking events become schmooze-fests where you spend two hours getting bombarded by people running around the room as if there is a prize for giving out the most handshakes, forced smiles, and business cards.

Networking events can be an absolutely marvelous way to create meaningful connections and start the process of building mutually beneficial relationships, but there is an art to it. I've got three great tips for you to take the schmooze out of networking.

Even if you don't attend networking events (although after this chapter you may want to), you can apply all of the information in this chapter to meet up groups, singles events, work parties, and social gatherings.

Ask Interesting Follow-Up Questions

Yes, we are still talking about asking questions, because it is such a powerful conversational tool. In Chapter 7 we discussed in depth why you should ask relevant questions, and we still want to do that here. But here we take it a step further and try very hard to ask *interesting* questions.

What counts as an interesting question? Any question that you don't get asked on a regular basis.

Do not ask: "How did you get into that?"

This is the follow-up question you'll be asked by every person you meet, and probably find yourself asking every person you meet, after finding out what they do for a living.

"I'm Brian."

"Hey Brian, I'm Paul. So, what do you do?"

"I'm a magician."

"Wow! How did you get into that?"

It doesn't have to be an unusual job like magic. "Receptionist? How did you get into that?"

It's the networking equivalent of talking about the weather: an easy question that is always relevant and gets the conversation started. While I am in favor of any question that starts a conversation, I am a bigger fan of interesting questions that shake up the routine.

Instead ask: "What do you love about [insert job/career]?"

This question does two things. First, it surprises your conversational partner with a question that they weren't expecting. They were ready to answer, "How did you get into that?" They might even start answering the wrong question!

It's kind of like when you think your friend is going to ask, "How are you?" and instead they ask, "What are you up to?"

You start to say, "I'm good, how are you?" and probably get out most of it before your brain catches up and realizes that something different is happening. It wakes you up, the same way that a great punchline or a terrific magic trick does.

Asking "What do you love about your job?" is disruptive in a good way, by keeping the conversation present instead of letting it coast on autopilot.

Second, the answer to this question reveals our values and beliefs. Even if you don't love your job, there is definitely *something* that you love about it. The more you can learn about a person's values and beliefs the better you can understand their perspective, which leads to stronger and more meaningful connections.

Put Away Your Business Cards

I have two different pockets at every networking event. The pocket for business cards I asked for, and the pocket for business cards that were handed to me, unsolicited.

Guess which pocket is always heavier at the end of the night?

The worst offender at networking events is the person who hands out their business card before they've even introduced themselves. Sometimes they actually hand out their card *instead of* introducing themselves.

I don't want to learn your name from your business card. I don't want to learn what you do from your business card. I don't want your business card unless I want your business card!

Do Not: Hand out your business card.

When you walk up and hand me your card before you have introduced yourself and at the very least learned my name, I feel like the only thing you're interested in is my business, my contacts, or my money. That may not be true, but remember, it doesn't matter what your intentions are.

Comedian Mitch Hedberg once quipped, "When someone hands me a flyer it's like they're saying, "Here. You throw this away.""

That's how I feel when someone hands me their card unsolicited. I put it in my left pocket and it stays there until I can find a garbage. It matters how you make me feel. And this makes me feel like garbage, so that's where your card goes.

Instead: Wait for someone to ask for your business card.

This is about quality over quantity. If you walk around the event handing out your card to everybody, then yes,

Don't hand out your card instead of introducing yourself.

they will all have your card. But how many of them will even remember whose card it was when they go through the stack later? Hardly anybody, and what good does that do you?

While it is polite and unassuming to wait for someone to ask for your card, it is also a more powerful first step to making a connection because you know that they actually want your information. That means you can follow up with confidence that you aren't being intrusive or annoying. It means that they want to hear from you.

But the question becomes, how do you get someone to ask for your business card?

Talk About Your Values

After discussing the weather, the first thing most people say when they meet someone new, particularly in networking events, is their job title.

Unless *right now* I need to hire someone who does exactly what you do, which is incredibly unlikely because if I did I probably would have already done that, then your job title alone doesn't mean that much to me. I probably have to ask, "What is that?" or "So, what exactly do you do?" in order to continue the conversation. What typically follows is a description of the roles of that job. The problem is this: the same description would apply to anybody who holds your job title. The conversation is headed down a path that is completely impersonal, which is the opposite of building a connection.

Instead of opening with a job title that leads into a generic description of said job, try opening the conversation by talking about your values. What do you believe in? What drives you? What about your job allows you to achieve those beliefs and values, and pursue whatever it is that you care about?

Simon Sinek started a modern revolution in the corporate world when he discovered and started teaching the concept of "The Why." His idea, presented in a now famous TED talk entitled "Start with Why," is that all companies know what they do. Some know how they do it. But very few know why they do it. He passionately argues that companies should reverse the order of information: start with why they do what they do, then explain how they do it, and then finally talk about what their product or service is.

Here's how he describes it in terms of Apple, the go-to example for innovative and influential companies that stand out from the rest. Most companies would present the information in this order:

- We make great computers.

- They're beautifully designed and user friendly.

- Want to buy one?

That represents the typical way companies engage in marketing. They start with what they do, move to how they do it, and rarely tell you why they do it. Instead, Apple presents the information in this order:

- In everything we do, we believe in challenging the status quo and thinking differently.

- Because we believe in challenging the status quo, we make our products beautifully designed and user friendly.

- We happen to make great computers.

- Want to buy one? (Sinek, 2010)

By reversing the order of information, it makes their ideal customers want to buy from them, regardless of what they are selling. As Simon points out, that's why we are not only comfortable buying computers from Apple, but also MP3 players, DVRs, and other devices we don't typically associate with a computer company. Because all of their products are driven by a purpose. The product itself becomes almost irrelevant to their customers. People who love Apple will buy anything they release because they love Apple.

I have found great success in similarly reversing the order of information during networking events and in all of my interpersonal communication. My ability to connect with people is best when I don't lead with "I'm a magician." Instead, I talk about my values and beliefs. Here's how I would order the information as a networking event:

I believe that everyone should feel heard, understood, and valued.

I work with people and organizations on creating events that connect, engage, and entertain their guests in a positive and meaningful way.

By the way, I'm a magician and a speaker.

When I stopped introducing myself as a magician and started talking about my beliefs, values, and passions, I found I was creating strong connections very quickly with precisely the kind of people I wanted to do business with. My clients hire me because they connect with me and share my vision. Those are the kind of people you want to attract at networking events.

Talk about your values instead of your job and you will find that people ask for your business card. They want your card so that they can form a relationship *with you*, regardless of your job title.

But what if you aren't sure what your values and beliefs are?

Let's work on that.

CHAPTER 13

Know Thyself

I regularly attend entertainment industry conferences where buyers and artists in a particular market meet for a few days. The advantage for buyers is they get to experience and interact with dozens of the finest live entertainers from across the country. This helps them determine which acts they may want to book for their audience in the coming year.

The advantage for artists is, of course, to be in room full of hundreds of buyers with their wallets out, ready to book entertainment for the next year.

One such organization that holds these conferences is NACA, the National Association for Campus Activities. College campus entertainment was one of my most lucrative markets before I shifted into the corporate world. Successful college market artists will tell you that the key to "making it" in the cutthroat field of campus entertainment is attending and, ideally, showcasing at the many regional NACA conferences and the annual national conference.

Most artists who attend NACA conferences only ever get to sell from a booth. If you've ever been to a wedding expo, you know exactly what it looks like. These chaotic "Marketplace" sessions often seem like a struggle for life itself. Hundreds of artists desperately vie for the attention of a thousand-or-so broke, sleep-deprived students from across the region as they rush around the conference floor in search of booths giving out the best freebies. From pins to t-shirts to ice cream to CDs—everyone is trying to out-freebie each other.

But if you're very lucky, you might get to showcase.

A NACA showcase is a 10-minute slot on stage in front of the entire conference to put your best work on display. Hundreds of artists from across the country submit (which costs hundreds of dollars, non-refundable whether you are accepted or not) for a slot, of which 30 or so are selected per conference.

Musicians take the 10-minute opportunity to play three songs, usually one original tune sandwiched in between two popular covers. Slam poets do their three best poems, often two humorous poems with a serious one sandwiched in between. Comedians do their best extended late-night set (the set list you would do if you ever got invited on to a popular talk show).

Magicians generally have a harder time than the rest. Our agents push us to do the largest number of tricks possible in under 10 minutes, while we delicately try to explain that magic tricks require set-ups that take time, without which the climax of the trick doesn't make any sense. In a strange twist that underscores the pressure of showcases, agents are often less interested in the limits of reality than magicians are.

Just beneath the surface of blood-thirsty artists seeking bookings lies the heart and soul of NACA conferences: networking and building connections.

Artists and agents work to build relationships with advisors and students during the Marketplace sessions, and artists build comradery with each other during meal breaks and after-hours hangouts. Cutthroat though the industry may be, and contrary to the popular "dueling magicians" trope that makes for great cinema, magicians tend to bond rather easily. If for no other reason, magicians are bound by the act of secret-keeping: the only people magicians are allowed to talk to about magic are other magicians.

I'll never forget the 2012 NACA Northeast regional conference held in Connecticut.

I was feeling pretty good after having given a successful showcase that, unbeknownst to me at the time, would lead to the most lucrative booking season from a single conference in my career (at that point). Upon returning from coffee and catching up with some other magical entertainers who I rarely get to see in person, we noticed a large group of eight or so magicians sitting in a circle in the lobby of the convention center. As we approached the group it was clear that they were engaged in some sort of debate.

Magicians, like practitioners in any field, are prone to lively debate over aspects of the industry. Amateur magicians are apt to debate over technique, while professional magicians are more likely to debate performance theory.

Before I could even hear what the discussion was about, it was clear that this was a theory debate.

"Miller! You studied philosophy—get over here," my friend Mat exclaimed as he noticed us walking up.

"What's up, guys?" I asked.

The round table consisted of many of the most talented and successful magicians in the industry. It was also clear that Mat was defending himself against the entire gang.

"Okay," he said to me, "So here's the question. Cards Across: good trick or bad trick?"

"Cards Across" is a classic of magic in which two volunteers are pulled from the audience and stand on opposite sides of the stage. One volunteer is asked to count ten cards and hold them tightly between their hands, and the other is asked to do the same. Then, magically, two or three cards transport from one volunteer's pile to the other's. Each volunteer counts their cards out loud for proof.

So, here was Mat's question: Is Cards Across a good trick or a bad trick?

"Sorry Mat," I laughed. "I know you do it in your show, but you asked the wrong guy. I've always hated Cards Across."

"No!" he exclaimed, before launching into a passionate defense of the plot, referencing famous magicians who have done it successfully.

I, and others, argued that making a few cards transport from one person to another simply isn't a powerful enough trick to warrant inclusion in a stage show, when there are so many incredible, mind-blowing card tricks to choose from. He argued that it had a lot of comedy potential, to which we all agreed, but counter-argued that he asked if it was a good magic trick, not if it had potential for comedy.

Mat defended himself against a room full of the best and most successful magicians in the country for at least 20 minutes before the debate ran its natural course and we all moved on, nobody's mind having been changed.

Two years later Mat performed his version of "Cards Across" on national television. He now performs it every night from his own sold-out theater in Las Vegas after becoming the first magician in history to win America's Got Talent.

Here's the point. Everyone in that fateful debate believed they knew better than Mat. But Mat knew something no one in that room of experts knew: Mat knew himself. And he rode his self-awareness past all of us right to the top of the field.

Who Are You, Really?

Mat taught me a valuable lesson: *It is impossible to connect with others if you don't understand who you are.*

As an interactive entertainer it is my job to connect with the audience every night, no matter who they are, what their varied backgrounds may be, or how many people are in attendance. This is a job that many newcomers find difficult, and some never really succeed at. It is not uncommon for a young or beginner performer to have wild success one night, and terrible failure the next. This can even happen under the same conditions, in the same venue, doing the same material. Beginners are often perplexed or even angry when they fail a show after having such a great experience the night before.

"The audience sucked tonight."

Aspiring entertainers often attribute their failure to the audience. Blame is a basic human instinct when things go wrong, and in the case of a live performer, it is incredibly easy to follow the logic, i.e., "Last night in this club at 8:00 pm with an audience of 100 people I had an amazing show. Tonight, in the same club at 8:00 pm with an audience of 100 people I had a terrible show. The only thing that changed was the audience, so tonight's audience must have sucked, while last night's audience was great. It's not my fault!"

This is an instance of drawing the wrong conclusion from the right analysis. What was the only thing that changed from one night to the next? The audience! That's the right analysis. But the correct conclusion is that you connected with the audience the first night, while you failed to do so the second night.

As a young magician I came to the same incorrect conclusion many times. It hindered my development as an artist until I finally understood the fault was mine, and not the audience. You can only fix something when you have correctly identified the problem. The problem was not inconsistent audience reactions; that was just a natural consequence of the problem. The problem was that I was failing to connect with every audience.

But some nights were great! How do you explain that?

No two audiences are alike, in the same way that no two people are alike. You wouldn't interact with your grandmother the same way you that interact with your best friend. You wouldn't give a presentation to a group of CEOs the same way you would talk to a group of middle schoolers. And yet that's essentially what I was doing. By failing to treat each audience individually and instead barreling forward

No two people are alike.

with my act as if they weren't even in the room, it was inevitable I was going to win over some crowds and alienate others.

Two things brought about a change that would propel my career forward.

First, I discovered the real problem and admitted it was my fault. Not only did that allow me to develop a solution (because I was trying to solve the actual problem rather than an imagined one), but admitting fault meant that it was within my power to fix it, rather than blaming somebody else and hoping that they would fix it for me.

Second, I developed a solid understanding of the character I was playing on stage. If you do not know who you are, you cannot connect with an audience.

Most performers play a version of themselves on stage, often taking 2-3 key characteristics of their true selves and amplifying them to create a sort of easily accessible avatar for an audience.

It was only after creating, honing, and learning to understand my on-stage persona that I was finally able to start connecting meaningfully with the audience. I knew myself, which is something that sounds obvious, even automatic, but is in practice incredibly difficult to achieve (and an ongoing, ever-changing process). Having finally understood myself I was free to be more receptive to learning about my audience each night. This newfound freedom manifested in a variety of ways, including a ritual of meeting and greeting audience members in the first few rows before the show, rather than hiding backstage awaiting my grand, theatrical entrance.

The beauty of developing and improving myself on-stage is it had a profound effect on my "real life" off-stage. As I mentioned earlier, the character I played on stage was an idealized version of the kind of person I wished I could be. Through the years it occurred to me that there didn't have to be two completely different people inside of me, one I reserved for performances, and one I reverted to in real life. Rather, I could actually be the person I wished I was, and the stage version would just be a simplified and slightly exaggerated version of him. So, I took the techniques, skills, and understanding of myself I developed for the stage and applied them to my life outside of magic.

Finally, for the first time in my life, I knew myself, and it helped me connect to both audiences and to the people I interacted with every day.

I still dislike Cards Across.

But witnessing Mat's ability to stick to his convictions and play to his strengths in spite of all the opposition was a powerful reminder that I needed to get a better handle on who I was and what I wanted.

How to Discover Your True Self

"Be yourself" is common advice for dating, interviews, making friends, giving presentations, networking, and almost any situation in life. It is well-intentioned advice that usually doesn't help at all, because most of us don't have a clear understanding of who we are. To be honest, we don't spend a lot of time thinking about it.

I discovered who I really was through my stage performances, but you don't have to be playing a stage persona in order to gain a clearer understanding of who you are.

Here are some questions that a performer might answer about his persona/character in order to fully bring them to life on stage, that will also help you discover the truth about yourself:

What is my proudest moment or achievement?
Was it graduating with a degree, raising a child, buying a house, or that time you helped a stranger when no one was looking? Why are you so proud of it?

What do I want most out of life?
Great stories have an "I wish" scene towards the beginning. It is a moment when the main character discovers the thing they want to achieve, usually as a result of a failure or unfortunate circumstance. You are the main character in the story of your life. Have you had an "I wish" moment?

When was the last time I was truly happy?
It may have been earlier today, last month, or many years ago (although hopefully not that long). It may have only lasted minutes, or it could have gone on for weeks. Capture that moment in your imagination. What about it brought such joy?

What is my biggest worry this week? This month? This year?

Our anxieties reveal a lot about our priorities. When you look closely at your concerns you may discover thought patterns you were never aware of.

What compliment is my favorite to receive?

We all like to receive praise, but not all compliments are equal. Do you prefer to receive a compliment about your fashion, your wit, your thoughtfulness, your diligence, …?

What does my best friend (or closest relative) do that most annoys me?

If you knew it wasn't going to hurt their feelings, what do you wish you could tell your most treasured human that totally bothers you?

What is one weakness that I wish was a strength?

Is there something that you've always wanted to get better at but just haven't seemed to be able to, or haven't put in the time? What would it take to get there?

What is one weakness that I wish people/the world would stop telling me to improve?

No matter how much you don't want to do this thing, your friends, family, strangers on the internet, and blog posts keep telling you to improve it. Why don't you want to get better at it?

> **More of these kinds of questions available at**
> **www.ThreeNewPeople.com**

I suggest you write a short essay in response to each of these questions. Do you notice any common themes or narratives running through your different answers? Jot down 3-5 words, terms, or themes that come up more than once. These are likely the most prominent pieces of your personality.

Once you have that list of 3-5 themes that make up who you are, you have a choice. For each theme, do you want to double down and improve upon it, or change something about it?

When you truly understand yourself, you will be able to identify shared beliefs to bond over with others, and fundamental differences to overcome. Connection is not always about agreeing. It is about feeling heard, understood, and valued.

Understanding yourself leads to others understanding you, which helps you understand them.

When it clicks, it feels like magic.

CHAPTER 14

Human Connection is Magic

I believe that magic is about connecting with people. But more than that, I believe that human connection is like magic.

There is a feeling that comes over me when I make a meaningful connection with another person that is as powerful and profound as the most wonderful magic.

With your permission I'd like to explore that feeling and what it means to me. Everything I have described and suggested in this book is an earnest effort to seek out and create the feeling of magic in my daily interactions with people, and to show you how you can create these connections in your own life.

I hope that by now I have earned your trust as I wax poetic about the artform that showed me the way out of my isolation and opened up a world of opportunities in the form of beautiful people to meet and connect with on a daily basis.

What is the Goal of Creating Magic?

If you want to stump (or shut up) a room full of magicians, ask them the simple question, "What is magic?"

You would think such a fundamental question would be an easy thing for a magician to answer. Instead you'll find that most magicians fail to come up with anything resembling a coherent thought about the nature of magic.

> "What is magic? What do you mean, 'What is magic?' Magic is, uh, well I mean of course magic is, well you know, it's like when you do something that's impossible, and, I mean... *sigh*. I don't know."

You can learn how to dance without having explicitly defined what dancing is. Similarly, you can learn to paint, sing, or build bookshelves in spite of never defining painting, singing, or carpentry. It is a function of human nature that we are able to learn what a thing is through examples. At some point before your first dance lesson you were shown a dancer and told, "This is dancing." If you are then shown a singer and told, "This is singing," you start to understand the difference between dancing and singing, so on and so forth.

And yet there seems to be something different about magic.

Although I admit I may be biased, I am also practitioner of many other art forms including guitar, singing, stand-up comedy, public speaking, cartooning, photography, and videography. While each of these practices is special in their own way, magic is unlike anything else I have either practiced or witnessed.

Magic, like the other art forms I mentioned, is a form of entertainment. But where magic differs from the rest is entertainment is not magic's end goal. That magic is entertaining is simply a natural consequence of its structure.

So, what is the end goal of magic?

Magic is specifically designed to produce the feeling of childlike wonder, a stirring inside of you that anything is possible, and even our wildest dreams can be made real.

And isn't that also the purest, most ambitious goal of meeting new people? That anything is possible on the other side of that next connection? That this stranger holds the key to a better career or a happier life?

That somehow you will profoundly impact each other like a "meet cute" in a romantic comedy, or a random encounter with the hiring manager at the company of your dreams?

That you might meet your Zoe, who leads to life-changing career opportunities that result in your standing on a metaphorical stage in Pompeii?

Creating Conversational Magic

Just like you cannot expect someone to understand you if you do not understand yourself, you cannot create the feeling or experience of magic, either on stage as a magician or in your daily interactions, unless you understand what magic is.

Someone who does magic tricks but does not understand the purpose of magic is a trickster at best, and a con artist at worst. The same goes for people who learn "conversational tricks" but lack an understanding of meaningful, human connection.

A great magician is more than a trickster. Great magic does not leave people feeling tricked, fooled, or lied to. Rather, a true magician opens the door to endless possibilities that otherwise only exist in dreams or imagination.

The techniques in this book and its underlying philosophy create a conversational magic when applied to human interaction.

My personal definition of magic?

Magic is the moment of conscious conflict between knowledge and evidence.

The word 'conscious' is crucial here. Magic presents a conflict that you are actively aware of and yet don't know how to resolve. It is the moment you see something and think, "I know that isn't possible, but all of my available evidence tells me that it's happening anyway."

On the morning of that super early flight if you had asked me "What four words would change your life today?" I might have answered, "You won the lottery." If you told me that the four words were "I like your hat" I probably would have laughed and told you to buzz off. The idea that meeting a stranger on a plane who liked my fedora would so dramatically change the course of my life would have seemed impossible. In fact, it felt impossible, even as it was happening.

That internal conflict, that something I believed was impossible was actually happening, is the feeling of magic.

I approach every conversation like there is an impossible thing waiting to happen. That something incredible can come out of every chance encounter, and any routine interaction.

But we have to be open to it. And more than that, we have to create it.

Magic is a Shared Experience

When I was 19 years old my mentor once asked me, "Why magic?" If we're being honest, the question insulted me.

"Why magic?" I thought. "Because it's fun! Because I'm good at it! Because it helps me talk to people!"

Why magic? Why anything, then?

"You're very bright," he explained. "You're at college on scholarship. You're a talented musician. You're doing stand-up comedy. So, my question is, why magic and not those other things?"

Put that way, it was a fair question. I didn't have an answer at the time. In the twelve years since, however, I've discovered the reason I felt drawn to magic:

Magic is an equalizer.

Imagine organizing an audience where you sit a rich woman next to a poor man; a middle aged single mom next to a young married man with no kids; a white Christian man next to a black Buddhist woman next to a child from a 3rd world country. Almost any type of entertainment you put in front of them will alienate someone in the crowd. All art is subjective, and you can't hope to reach that many different kinds of people from those vastly assorted backgrounds in one shot.

Except magic.

Something incredible can come out of every chance encounter.

At the moment of magic, everybody goes to the same place: a childlike state of wonder. For a moment, and I mean *just* a moment, all of life's superficiality like race, religion, and socio-economic status disappear, and everybody is on the same playing field. Everybody is in the same emotional space.

That is what I strive to create in every conversation in my daily interactions: a shared experience.

Magic is universal. Impossible is impossible, no matter who you are or where you come from.

So too with people. Connection is connection, no matter who you are or where you come from.

We all dream, we are all curious, and we all yearn to be heard, understood, and valued.

Kids experience 'wonder' in its purest form and adults lose some of it as life's challenges and responsibilities weigh down upon us. A child doesn't care how much money you have or what race, religion, or gender you are. Such superficial ideas are learned through culture and circumstances.

Magic does the impossible: it erases those differences.

So too can a meaningful connection.

People Who Aren't Interested

"But Brian, some people just aren't interested in connecting."

I can't tell you how many times I've received that comment, Tweet, or email since the TEDx talk launched. My response is this:

The TEDx talk's title is "How to Magically Connect with *Anyone*," not "How to Magically Connect with *Everyone*."

Connection is a two-way street. It is a mutually beneficial exchange of emotional data. No matter how good your intentions are, or how well you learn, hone, and implement the techniques in this book, some people just aren't going to be open to connecting with you.

And that's okay.

Michael Jordan didn't win every game.

Steve Jobs didn't nail every product (Antennagate, anyone?).

You will not connect with every person you try to connect with.

The very best you can do is put all of yourself into the world. With each person, every day, give your very best effort to build a connection. If your best effort is rejected, then there's nothing to be upset about.

That person simply wasn't for you. Or you weren't for them. Or both.

It's not a quantity game. There's no scorecard that keeps track of how many people you made a meaningful connection with. The number doesn't matter. It's the quality of the relationships with the people you *have* connected with that matter.

What you might be concerned about is the breakdown of relationships with people who *were* willing to connect with you.

When Connections Break Down

Whether digital or in-person, miscommunications affect relationships differently depending on the strength and history of the relationship. A single language-based misunderstanding between Lindsey and myself is not going to break our relationship, no matter how frustrated I get over her pronunciation of 'crayon' as 'cran.' Our relationship has built up enough trust to survive that.

Even so, small missteps can build up over time. Like cracks in a sidewalk they can eventually break down even the strongest of relationships if you're not careful.

On the other hand, a seemingly silly or insignificant misunderstanding can absolutely take down a new relationship. I still don't know what my lovely blind date meant by "that explains it" when I informed her my accent was Buffalonian, but I wasn't going to stick around long enough to find out.

Have you ever made a joke with a new group of friends or colleagues, only to have it met with dead silence? You find yourself wondering if it offended them, if they didn't get it, or if they simply didn't find it funny.

Speaking of Lindsey, here's something that happened to me just a few months ago.

During a stage magic show in a college campus theater of about 800 students and their families, I invited a girl up on stage to assist with a trick. I take great care of my volunteers, refusing to make fun of them or put them in embarrassing situations. As we've discussed, it takes great courage to volunteer for a magic show and I do my best to treat people with respect in that vulnerable situation.

This girl was a freshman in college. I thanked her for volunteering and asked for her name.

She said, "Lindsey."

I instinctively responded, "That's my wife's name!"

The audience audibly and visibly turned on me, and it completely took me by surprise. It was a full three seconds of silence before I realized what had happened. Nobody in the audience knew that I was married and that my wife's name is Lindsey. From their perspective, it looked like I was hitting on an 18-year-old girl with an old-fashioned and wildly inappropriate pickup attempt.

The second I realized the misunderstanding I started waving my left hand around.

"No, no! I'm married!" I exclaimed, frantically pointing at my wedding band. "My wife's name is actually Lindsey!"

I tried to salvage the moment by finding common ground with her.

"Do you spell it with an 'a' or an 'e'?" I asked.

"An 'e'," she responded.

"Yeah, so does she! She always has trouble finding it spelled the right way on souvenirs."

The girl chuckled and said she did too. I went on with the trick, and the rest of the show went fine. But the spell had been broken. The first 10 minutes of the show until that incident had been raucous and energetic, and in the 50 minutes after it happened I never fully reconnected with the audience.

It was an honest and innocent misunderstanding, but it happened so early in our relationship that the audience didn't have enough history or trust built up with me to stay connected.

Should you try to reconnect if a relationship breaks down? It depends on your history and the circumstances.

As a performer with another 50 minutes of contracted stage time I had no choice but to try to reconnect and build the relationship back up.

If you suffer the breakdown of a relationship with a colleague or boss, and the success of your career depends on your ability to work well as a team, then it's probably a good idea to make every attempt to reconnect.

If it happens in your personal life, you'll have to weigh the potential outcomes of trying to reconnect. Not all relationships are meant to be or meant to last. Human connections are only healthy when both sides are emotionally invested in each other's well-being.

Sometimes the best thing you can do for yourself and others when a connection breaks down is to leave it alone.

Cherish the connection you had and learn from the breakdown. There's always a lesson, and there is always room for improvement.

In fact, my biggest, most regrettable failures in human connection led to this book.

CHAPTER 15

Three New People

At the very start of this book I told you a story about creating magic for a lovely man named Ed, who happened to be blind. I noted specifically that I didn't want him to feel tricked. In other words, I didn't want him to associate the experience of magic with the feeling of being taken, conned, or swindled.

Truthfully, that's how I feel about all of my magic.

I believe people are most receptive to new ideas when they feel like they are a part of the process rather than peering in from outside. It is possible to witness a magic trick without feeling stupid. You recognize there *is* a trick, but yourself do not feel tricked.

The real secret is creating that shared experience in which the magician and the audience are a part of something together, rather than facing off against each other. Under the right circumstances and in the right mindset we can be transported together.

The magician is the only person who cannot see the magic. We *must* immerse ourselves in the perspective of the audience in order to create wonder.

Connection works the same way.

I believe that we can create real magic in our daily interactions with friends, family, colleagues, clients, and even strangers. Magic is the moment of conscious conflict between knowledge and evidence. It is the moment when you know something is impossible, but your evidence tells you that it's happening anyway.

Most of us, myself included, go about our public lives with our guards up. You are not expecting a life-changing encounter during your routine trip to the grocery store for that avocado you forgot to buy. Further than that, you *know* it isn't possible for that to happen.

I believe that we can create real magic in our daily interactions with friends, family, colleagues, clients, and even strangers.

I certainly wasn't expecting a stranger to utter four words in the last seat of an airplane that would completely change the course of my life. I *knew* that wasn't possible.

But she did. A connection was formed, and a powerful relationship was born within what I believed were impossible conditions. In retrospect, that moment can only be described as pure magic.

I didn't know it then, but of course, I couldn't have.

Magic only exists in our memory. It takes our mind at least a few moments to juxtapose what actually happened with what we know before we can conclude that something impossible has taken place.

The same is true of our relationships, whether they are friendly, professional, or romantic. We cannot recognize the magic of a new connection or where it will lead until after it has already done so. We can only connect the dots looking back.

Real magic takes courage and confidence. You must step outside of your comfort zone and open yourself up to failure. It's so much easier to stick to small talk than it is to be open and vulnerable. Take a deep breath and try it. Just try it. The reward is worth the risk, I promise.

You don't have to learn a card trick to be a magician. You don't need to pull a rabbit out of a hat or pull a coin from an ear. You don't need white gloves or a cape or a tuxedo. You don't need a bunch of lame jokes, and you certainly don't need a wand.

True magic is not a trick. You can live every single day of your life with a magician's mindset: create shared experiences through impossible moments of connection.

Every single person you meet has a life completely unto themselves. They have hopes, dreams, worries, and concerns just as real and vivid as your own. Each of those people may have different belief systems, backgrounds, cultures, religions, languages, or ideologies.

At the end of your life you will have interacted with 80,000 individuals that are completely unique and yet fundamentally similar: they are all human beings who crave meaningful connections with others.

You meet an average of three new people every single day.

What will you do with your three opportunities today?

Thank you so much for your time reading *Three New People*.

If you enjoyed it, I would really appreciate if you could take just a few minutes to leave a review on Amazon. It can be rather short if you only have a moment.

Amazon seems to prioritize *quantity* of reviews when deciding how and when to suggest a book to users. More reviews will help readers like you find this book and re-discover the beauty and power of human connection.

Here's a direct link:
http://brianmillerspeaks.com/tnp-amazon-review

You have my gratitude.

~Brian

Acknowledgments

I would like to formally thank the following people who had a profound impact on the development of this book, either directly or indirectly.

Lindsey, my wife, best friend, and love of my life: for all the things.

My family – Dad, Mom, Mike, Emma - for your constant and unwavering support my entire life. You give me strength, and I channel it to pursue my wildest dreams and ambitions.

Grandma and Pa, for being my rock, and a phone call away no matter what. You embody "listening to understand."

Scott, Lindsey, Danny, Stephanie, and David at Neon Entertainment, for taking a chance on a 22-year-old know-it-all, growing my career from nothing, and giving me a safety net just wide enough to consistently leap from higher heights.

Tim, for investing your time and energy in me from afar, and your selflessness in an industry where secret-keeping is the norm.

Adam, for giving me undiluted and unabashedly honest feedback, even when I'm really not in the mood (because you know I really do want to hear it). You inspire and push me as you have since we were but 13 years old.

Kasey, for being my dear friend, and also, you know, for connecting me with Parag, who then gave me an opportunity to speak at a tiny TEDx conference. Who knew?

Parag, for giving me an opportunity to speak at a tiny TEDx conference. Who knew? Our local community owes you a debt of gratitude. What a gift you've given so many of us.

Mila, for designing such a beautiful cover and logo for the movement.

Melissa, my lovely editor, for pushing me to tighten my arguments and shape my writing into a consistent and compelling voice.

Nevin, for your help on the road. But more importantly, for reminding me why I got into this business in the first place. Your enthusiasm reignites my love of magic every time we talk.

Seth, for being my hero and teacher. Your relentless generosity and prolific output motivate me daily. That you set aside your precious time to read this book means everything. I'll never forget it.

Zoe, for being a rock star.

The *Three New People* pre-launch team: *Heatherlyn, Jonathan, Ian, Richard, Paul, Joe, Stephanie, Stephen, Ryan, Sarah, Ben, Danny, Kat, Amanda, Dennis, Jenna, Matt, Heather, Brandon, Shaun, Lou, Jenny, Elizabeth.* Your insightful feedback was crucial to the final stages of editing, design, and marketing of this project. I can't thank you enough for gifting me your time to help see this vision to the finish line.

References & Suggested Reading

Adam, H., & Galinsky, A. D. (2012, July). Enclothed cognition. *Journal of Experimental Social Psychology, 48*(4), 918-925.

Cain, S. (2013). *Quiet: The Power of Introverts in a World That Can't Stop Talking.* New York: Broadway Books.

Carnegie, D. (1998). *How to Win Friends and Influence People.* New York: Pocket Books.

Cigna U.S. Loneliness Index. (2018, May). Retrieved from Cigna: https://www.multivu.com/players/English/8294451-cigna-us-loneliness-survey/docs/IndexReport_1524069371598-173525450.pdf

Cuddy, A. (2012, June). *Your body language may shape who you are.* Retrieved from TED: https://www.ted.com/talks/amy_cuddy_your_body_language_shapes_who_you_are

Ducharme, J. (2018, February 28). *Using Your Phone At Dinner Isn't Just Rude. It Also Makes You Unhappy.* Retrieved from Time: http://time.com/5178352/phone-ruining-dinner/

Epley, N. (2014). *Mindwise: How We Understand What Others Think, Believe, Feel, and Want.* New York: Vintage Books.

Godin, S. (2012). *The Icarus Deception.* New York: Portfolio. Retrieved from ChangeThis: https://changethis.com/manifesto/100.01.IcarusDeception/pdf/100.01.IcarusDeception.pdf

Haydn, W. (2012). *Stories of a Street Performer: Memoirs of a Master Magician.* Los Angeles: Mikazuki Publishing House.

Koenig, J. (n.d.). *Sonder.* Retrieved from The Dictionary of Obscure Sorrows: http://www.dictionaryofobscuresorrows.com/post/23536922667/sonder

Kubo, C., & Machado, A. (2017, June 1). *The Science is Clear: Why Multitasking Doesn't Work.* Retrieved from Cleveland Clinic: https://health.clevelandclinic.org/science-clear-multitasking-doesnt-work/

List of awards and nominations received by Ellen DeGeneres. (2018, August 9). Retrieved from Wikipedia: https://en.wikipedia.org/wiki/List_of_awards_and_nominations_received_by_Ellen_DeGeneres

Seidman, R. (2010, November 9). *Syndicated Rates: Oprah Still Ahead of Judge Judy; Monk Lives On.* Retrieved from https://tvbythenumbers.zap2it.com/sdsdskdh279882992z1/syndicated-ratings-oprah-still-ahead-of-judge-judy-monk-lives-on/71424/

Sinek, S. (2010). *How great leaders inspire action.* Retrieved from TED: https://youtu.be/qp0HIF3SfI4

Slepian, M. L., Ferber, S. N., & Gold, J. M. (2015, March 31). The Cognitive Consequences of Formal Clothing. *Social Psychological and Personality Science, 6*(6), 661-668.

The Psychology of Eye Contact, Digested. (2016, November 28). Retrieved from The British Psychological Society: https://digest.bps.org.uk/2016/11/28/the-psychology-of-eye-contact-digested

Traffic Safety Facts. (2016, September). Retrieved from National Highway Safety Traffic Administration: https://www.nhtsa.gov/sites/nhtsa.dot.gov/files/documents/driver_electronic_device_use_in_2015_0.pdf

About the Author

Brian Miller is a corporate keynote speaker, youth motivational speaker, and magician. For 12 years he has shared his magic and his message with thousands of audiences in 11 countries across 4 continents.

As a child, Brian suffered from a debilitating social and speech anxiety. He was bullied and mostly friendless through middle school. Though he loved magic tricks, he couldn't muster the courage to perform for anyone. Brian got a fresh start in a new school for 9th grade, where he met another student who was also into magic. Together they studied magic and encouraged each other to perform for their classmates and teachers. Through magic, Brian developed self-confidence for the very first time.

Founding his business at the early age of 16, Brian worked as a professional magician while completing a dual Bachelor of Science in mathematics and philosophy, achieving a 4.0 in philosophy and receiving two international awards for presenting original work. He was accepted into a PhD program for Philosophy of Language but turned it down in order to pursue a career in entertainment.

Brian quickly found a following with college students on the national campus activities circuit, earning two nominations for "America's Best Campus Artist" (Campus Activities Magazine) by the age of 24.

As his act evolved, so did the demand for his work. Brian developed a reputation for mixing world class entertainment with an engaging personality and the ability to adapt to any group. He began accepting invitations to entertain at exclusive private events throughout New England.

Eventually Brian began receiving invitations for speaking engagements. In 2015 the global success of his TEDx talk "How to Magically Connect with Anyone" propelled him into the world of corporate keynote speaking and youth motivational speaking, where he now spends most of his time.

Brian lives in Connecticut, USA with his wife Lindsey.

Sign up for weekly email tips on connecting at:
www.ThreeNewPeople.com

www.BrianMillerSpeaks.com

www.BrianMillerMagic.com

CPSIA information can be obtained
at www.ICGtesting.com
Printed in the USA
LVHW042114211119
638113LV00006B/1062/P